a/w

INCOME FOR LIFE

INCOME
for LIFE

THE RETIREE'S GUIDE TO
CREATING INCOME FROM SAVINGS

S. Joseph DiSalvo, ChFC, AIF
& Marie L. Madarasz, AIF

LIONCREST
PUBLISHING

INCOME FOR LIFE

The Retiree's Guide to Creating Income From Savings

ISBN   978-1-5445-0317-2 *Hardcover*

       978-1-5445-0318-9 *Paperback*

       978-1-5445-0319-6 *Ebook*

To our clients—whose wisdom, visions of the future, and commitment to following a plan continues to inspire and motivate us to keep learning and improving.

And to our families, with much love!

CONTENTS

INTRODUCTION

Between the years of 1946 and 1964, seventy-six million babies were born in the United States; today, the baby boomer generation represents nearly a quarter of the American population. At this moment, these seventy-six million Americans are on the verge of retirement—and some have already passed that threshold. Americans are now retiring earlier than any other time in history, with the average retirement age currently sitting at sixty-three, and millions opting to retire even earlier, in their late fifties. Concurrently, Americans are now living longer than they ever have before.

The confluence of these sociological shifts has created a landscape of uncharted territory for those about to retire. What income, precisely, can be expected or counted upon? What kind of preparation and planning will be required? Exactly how much money will one need for a retirement that lasts thirty or forty years, rather than ten or twenty?

If you're among those feeling uncertainty about your financial future as you move into retirement, you are the person for whom we wrote this book.

It's natural, and even reasonable, to have myriad questions about how to prepare for retirement. Are you financially prepared for this transition? How much will you be able to spend each year? What will happen when the stock market takes an inevitable future downturn? Will you be able to maintain your current standard of living? The baby boomers, after all, are the healthiest, most active aging demographic the country has ever seen. In contrast to earlier generations, baby boomers have more money and are accustomed to spending more money. They are also known broadly as the "sandwich generation"; many baby boomers simultaneously care for both their elderly parents and their cash-strapped children.

This creates a somewhat scattered puzzle to assemble as retirement approaches. Many of our clients come to us with a host of questions that reveal a lack of confidence in their ability to maintain the strong self-reliance ingrained into them by their Depression-raised, WWII-forged parents. Deep knowledge of personal financial planning is uncommon among the general population. Personal financial education is essentially nonexistent; there are few "personal finance" courses offered in high school or college, even though a basic foundation of knowledge in that discipline is possibly the most important thing we can teach our children to ensure that they will not just survive as adults, but thrive.

Without that basic foundation, it's no wonder that many retirement-age Americans feel deeply unsettled, and even afraid, of what comes next. And without the context of financial literacy, it's nearly impossible to make decisions in the face of shifting social security and Medicare policy, and the de-prioritization of pensions in favor of what is referred to as a Defined Contribution Plan, i.e., 401(k), 403(b) etc. The retirement landscape that baby boomers must prepare to navigate is simply not the same world their parents lived in. Some anxiety is to be expected.

That's why we wrote this book. This fear can be mostly overcome with a straightforward education of the basics and practical tools to help you plan for the road ahead. Throughout our careers, which span a combined forty years, we've helped hundreds of clients (and thousands of others through our workshops) like yourself build confidence and security in their upcoming retirement; we're eager now to share this wealth of knowledge with you, and help you envision your future as one not of uncertainty, but of opportunity, and even abundance.

PLAN FOR YOUR FUTURE

Where should you begin your retirement planning? With so many elements of socioeconomic change at play, so many pieces of the puzzle to sort and organize, and so much at stake, what starting point makes the most sense?

Unlike previous generations, who were able to rely on the primary safety nets of social security benefits and pensions when defining and mapping their post-retirement income and spending, baby boomers are best served by learning the fundamentals of investing and the fundamentals of converting their savings to an ongoing, growing income stream. This is not to diminish the potential impact of a good social security decision. Planned well, a good social security claiming decision will easily represent tens or hundreds of thousands of dollars of additional income in retirement. However, social security planning deals with a static source; once you've made your decision and executed that part of your plan, for the most part, it's done.

By contrast, your investments, and how you go about converting those investments into income, represents an ongoing opportunity to a continuously growing income stream; as such, a solid and well-planned investment and income strategy is where you'll create the greatest impact on your retirement. It's been our experience that most people lack confidence when it comes to investing.

Some may consider themselves unlucky in the market (when, in reality, they've probably just been receiving the wrong advice), or others may write themselves off entirely, chalking up their lack of investment knowledge to the idea that investing is a specialized skill they never learned and will probably never understand.

Even those who made good investments over the course of their working years with an eye toward retirement may feel burned by the recent market events in 2008 and the resulting recession. They may have lost a sizeable portion of their safety net, and along with it, their confidence.

Our goal with this book is to rebuild or create from scratch that confidence so that you can feel safe, not fearful, as your retirement approaches. We'll give you the tools to make informed choices, and we'll deliver the clarity you're seeking in the form of accessible, practical exercises that will build your skills in retirement income planning.

By the time you've finished reading this book, you'll have a clear idea of how to organize your finances and how to develop an impactful investment and income strategy. We'll answer the most common questions we've heard about retirement planning, which are probably most of the questions you've accumulated, as well. You'll learn how to focus on what you can control versus what you can't—and you'll learn how to distinguish between the two. You'll be far better prepared to know what further questions to ask if you choose to work with whomever you choose to work with, whether they be a discount broker, a full-service broker, or a true financial advisor—and you'll gain insight into how those roles differ, and what kind of advice you should seek.

Put simply, you'll come out the other side of this book exponentially better-informed, better-prepared, and our hope is far more confident. Most importantly, you'll be in a strong position to make informed choices that will have a positive impact on your future.

MASTERING THE FUNDAMENTALS

We constructed this book to be a straightforward, accessible education in how to invest your savings to create a growing stream of income in retirement. Our aim is to help you get organized and provide you with a strong foundation for creating your retirement income strategy.

We also intend to show you that preparing for your retirement is simpler than you may assume—it takes work and a little bit of personal responsibility, but it's not the labyrinth most people think it is. The blame for this misconception can be largely laid at the feet of the American news media, in which personal finance has been packaged largely as entertainment. Soon-to-be-retirees tune in to financial news shows hoping for a hint about what they should do with their money, and instead, they're bombarded with out-of-context, sensationalized content that provides little in the way of actionable information. What action is one expected to take in response to upcoming trends in oil prices? How does that provide a retiree with a clear direction forward?

By contrast, we've kept this book focused. Our aim is to provide you with context and clarity on what will matter most to your retirement: converting savings to income.

What this book *isn't* is a comprehensive, exhaustive guide to each and every aspect of retirement income planning. There are countless books and resources that can guide you through the intricacies of tax planning, estate planning, insurance planning, and the numerous details of social security and Medicare planning. We'll touch on some of the other fundamentals of retirement income planning, like social security, taxes, and spending, but for the most part, we've kept the focus where it belongs: building your confidence in the basics of what will create the biggest financial impact in the years ahead, which is how you go about converting your savings to income.

A LIFETIME OF EXPERIENCE; A LANDSCAPE OF OPPORTUNITY

Over the combined forty years we've served in the financial planning industry, we've watched markets go up and down, trends come and go, financial services multiply with complexity, and disruptions like technology change the face of the industry. Our own knowledge and skill sets have evolved alongside the ever-changing dynamics of the business. Through it all, though, the primary needs and wants of most people remain the same: people need to feel secure in their future, and they want to live out their retirement decades in happiness, health, and comfort.

That's why we decided to keep this book simple and aimed to serve the needs of people like the thousands of clients and workshop attendees we've advised. Empowering people with the knowledge they need to make good choices with their money will always be the most satisfying part of our careers. Our intention is to inspire you to a state of planning, control, knowledge, and forward motion.

At the time of this writing, both authors are in our fifties. We understand what it feels like to be facing retirement, and we understand that it can appear foreboding, like uncharted territory. We've been in the industry long enough to know what works, and what doesn't; our experience is a map through that uncharted territory, and we're eager to bring you along.

When social security was enacted in 1935, the average American's life expectancy was fifty-seven. Today, it's eighty-three. It is an unprecedented event in our country for its largest demographic to be almost entirely composed of retirees, but unprecedented doesn't necessarily mean unpredictable. Feeling unprepared for retirement is entirely reasonable; fear, though, doesn't have to color your planning. Understanding the fundamentals of retirement income planning isn't a matter of aptitude, it's a matter of education. This book will help provide that.

Put simply, if you don't know what you don't know, the first step is to learn. Join us as we uncover the basic financial knowledge that will empower you to make the right decisions with your money, begin to pull together a basic retirement income plan, and position yourself to create income for life.

Part One

PUTTING RETIREMENT INCOME INTO FOCUS

CHAPTER ONE

THE RIGHT MINDSET FOR THE BIG TRANSITION

Recently, we met with a prospective client who seemed, on the surface, to be well-prepared for retirement. He was in his early sixties and had responsibly saved his income throughout his working years; by the time he started planning his retirement transition, he had well over a million dollars in his 401(k), a small pension and social security.

When we began working with him during that first meeting, though, we discovered that the majority of his savings was in cash, CDs, and bonds. As we'll explain in great detail later in this book, this type of very conservative allocation can represent an unnecessary challenge to the investor who needs to create a growing stream of income for upwards of thirty years!

This client had had the best of intentions, but he simply was operating with an outdated perspective. He'd followed the popular wisdom passed on to him by his parents and put his money in "safe" places, avoiding the volatility of the financial markets. In reality, he had unknowingly set up himself and his family for an income that will become increasingly difficult, if not impossible, to keep up with inflation.

"Have you given any thought to investing a portion of your money to stocks?" we asked him.

"Oh, no, I couldn't do that," he told us. "What if the market crashes? I'll lose everything."

This client was petrified of the mere notion of investing in the stock market. He was immensely distrustful of what he saw as a volatile and rigged system, and without any real education in how to handle his investment portfolio, he'd unwittingly made himself and his family vulnerable to two of the long-term risks a retiree faces: inflation risk and longevity risk, which we will discuss in depth later on.

Moreover, this client isn't the first we've seen with this confused and fearful mindset—not by a long shot. If anything, his mindset is shared by many people nearing retirement.

WHERE DID THIS MINDSET COME FROM?

By and large, people operate in a fear-based mindset when it comes to their money, and especially when it comes to their retirement income. Some people might not be *afraid*, necessarily, just confused, because they lack basic financial literacy; but that confusion still leads them to make the same bad decisions as their more fearful cohort. For instance, they'll invest their money in less risky assets in order to be "safe" or, arguably worse, they'll pull their money out of the *right* places prematurely because they're worried it'll be lost.

Why does this fear-based mindset seem to be the norm among many of the baby boomer-aged retirees? There are multiple historical and social factors that have converged to create a common atmosphere of confusion and trepidation. Understanding the root causes of this mindset is crucial to take steps toward changing it.

DEPRESSION-ERA PARENTS

It's true for almost everyone: much of what people know about money, they learned from their parents.

The current generation of retirees and soon-to-be retirees had parents who were raised during the aftermath of the Great Depression. This experience made an immense formative impact on them and created a scarcity mindset.

To a Depression-era person, the worst possible thing that could happen to someone was losing all their money.

Those who lived through the Great Depression's aftermath also largely shared a common misconception about the cause of the event; most people were convinced that the Depression was the result of the stock market crash of 1929. In reality, the crash of 1929 was just one factor among several, and not at all the root or even primary cause of the economic situation the country found itself in.

The parents of the baby boomer generation had the best of intentions, but were, for the most part, operating from a skewed guidebook when they passed on their financial knowledge to their children. As a result, some of them inadvertently raised adults who are distrustful of the stock market and so worried about losing all their money that they neglect to invest it in the ways that would serve them best.

LITTLE FINANCIAL EDUCATION

As we discussed in the introduction, the United States education system suffers from a glaring lack of attention to personal finance. It's exceedingly rare for high schools, let alone university-level institutions, to offer students courses on personal finance; most would-be adults walk the stage at their college graduation without any idea how to manage their money, and certainly very little sense of the fundamentals of portfolio management, let alone how to create an income from a portfolio of stocks, bonds, and cash.

With such a paucity of information on such a critical subject, most adults simply follow conventional wisdom throughout their working years. They follow the prescription laid out by their parents, general rules of thumb, and the financial-media celebrities. This, as we'll explain next, is not a formula that sets anyone up for financial success.

MEDIA MISINFORMATION

The financial media, including many cable news and print publications, do the public an enormous disservice in their focus on short-term financial projections. Worse, fear-based reporting is amplified in the existing worried mindset of retirement-aged people, and as a result, they're more likely to latch on to reactionary advice that is likely irrelevant to their particular financial situation.

Financial news organizations inadvertently express to their audience that the two most important aspects of investing to focus on are *timing* and *selection*.

Timing is exactly what it sounds like: when it's good to

get into the market, and when it's good to get out; or, less obviously, when one should over-weight or under-weight a particular type of investment. Put simply, *timing* refers to when a consumer investor should buy or sell investments. Selection is also what it sounds like—*should I pick Google over Amazon? Is Microsoft a better pick than Apple?* For day traders, people whose job it is to make as much short-term profit as possible for clients, timing and selection are certainly of primary concern. But the vast majority of the financial media's audience does not consist of day traders, and in fact is made up of people looking to maximize their long-term financial resources to fund real-life long-term goals. Although these kinds of discussions can sell air time and magazines and drive commissions, they have very little impact on investor results long-term.

We often talk with prospective clients who recount to us how fearful they felt during the financial crisis of 2008, and how they made decisions in hindsight that cost them a lot of money. If we can agree that the financial media concentrates too much on timing and selection, we can also make the case for the *general* media skewing the news toward an "end of the world" mentality. They are forever crying foul and focusing on what's going wrong versus what's going right. Think back to 2008, particularly after the collapse of Lehman Brothers; what we heard from the media was, "The world as we know it is going to end! The sky is falling!"

At what point in history have we sustained a real crisis that does not eventually work itself out? Human nature is programmed to more easily believe bad news, and be skeptical of good news—hence the famous saying, "Human nature is a failed investor." But how does this media hype help *anyone* make the best decisions that are consistent with their real-life, long-term goals?

INDUSTRY CHALLENGE

It's incumbent upon us to bring up an important subject: in the decade since the financial crisis of 2008, we have had time to look back and assess what transpired and what has changed. Lasting damage occurred on many fronts, not least of which was a serious erosion of trust in the financial services industry—and deservedly so. Our industry as a whole continues to fall short of delivering on what consumers really need and want: financial service professionals who can consistently offer value to clients by demonstrating professionalism and providing solutions, not simply pushing products. And for those investors in or on the verge of retirement, having a choice of professionals who focus on retirement income planning and who will address their individual needs becomes vitally important; most importantly, those professionals should provide unbiased advice that cuts through the noise, thereby helping their clients mitigate unforced errors and emotional decision-making.

A primary reason why we wrote this book is precisely to address this issue. Our goal is to make up for some of the informational gaps that exist, and for this book to be a trusted resource for an entire generation of people who haven't been offered the guidance and information they so dearly need in order to comfortably and confidently live out their coming decades of retirement.

RATIONAL FEARS

By no means do we want to create the impression that people who exhibit a fear-based mindset are suffering from *irrational* fears; on the contrary, their fears are highly rational.

Many clients who seek our advice, for example, saw their financial portfolio suffer greatly as a result of the recession of 2008, and the fear of that time still resonates. They saw their account values drop anywhere from twenty-five to fifty percent. They've formed a recency bias when it comes to their opinion of the stock market; having been, as they feel, so recently burned, they're reluctant to again go near what they perceive to be a dangerous flame.

This is completely rational. Who wouldn't be leery, having been through such a damaging market event so recently?

What we want to make clear is that the fears people have about their retirement income aren't irrational. It's the decisions they make as a result of those fears that can be irrational, depending on how short-term and reactionary their outlook becomes.

As we'll show in detail later in this book, even a market event as impactful as that of 2007–2009 can be managed to some extent, as long as a retiree has a well-formulated plan and commits to sticking to that plan no matter what day-to-day worries arise.

THE KEY TO CONFIDENCE: DEVELOP A PLAN

To make good decisions, it's vitally important to educate oneself on the basics of planning income for retirement, and use that knowledge to build a strong long-term plan.

What we've seen in our many years in this industry is that, once a plan is in place, people's mindsets change from fear and confusion to *confidence*. That confidence is an important component of a successful retirement.

A client of ours, Gary, had accumulated enough resources during his working years that, by the time he began planning his retirement with us, he had three million dollars to work with. Even with that sum at his disposal, when asked if he felt confident about his retirement income, he always answered: "We *should* be okay."

It's rare that a person, even one as well-prepared as Gary, exhibits confidence in their retirement finances. The answer is never, "Yes, we'll definitely be okay!" It's usually something more along the lines of, "I think we should be okay."

On some level, retirees without a plan are simply *guessing* that they'll have enough money for the rest of their lives, and there is very rarely any confidence in that guess.

We worked with Gary to create a comprehensive and well-thought-out income plan for his retirement. Once we showed him in detail where his income was going to come from, how his resources were going to be distributed, and how his plan would be able to weather any inevitable market downturn, Gary gained assurance in his ability to retire successfully. He suddenly looked at his retirement with confidence, where once there were ambiguity and anxiety.

It had nothing to do with the amount of money he had; it all came down to the plan. Once the plan was in place, Gary followed it to the letter. He's now enjoying every moment of his retirement, comfortable in his income and confident in the coming decades.

FROM CHALLENGE TO OPPORTUNITY

Retirement will happen one way or another; to make it as successful and fulfilling as possible, actively planning for it must be the top priority as one heads into the transition. The bottom line is that retirement, for all that it can seem like an enormous, confusing challenge, is actually an enormous opportunity if one is smart, dedicated, and willing to change their mindset.

It's critical to commit to educating oneself on the basics of retirement income planning so that potential future income isn't lost to ignorant mistakes. It's also important to understand when to ask for help and seek the advice of professionals, if needs be. Having a rock-solid plan in place is the key to confidence, knowledge, and well-set expectations are the recipe for success once the transition to retirement is complete.

MAKING THE TRANSITION

The transition into retirement is one of the biggest and most impactful transitions of a person's life. The only bigger transition, in fact, is the eventual decline of health that goes with the progression toward old age. With a mindset of preparation and confidence, the transition into retirement will be much smoother and less stressful for the retiree, but that doesn't mean the transition itself is easy.

When a person moves from decades in the working world, with so much of their time and even their identity wrapped up in their career, to the post-career state of retirement, they go through more than just a financial transition. They endure an emotional transition as well, and it's vitally important to acknowledge and prepare for that transition even as income plans are being put into place.

FROM ACCUMULATION TO DISTRIBUTION

The two phases of one's financial life, *accumulation* (the saving years) and *distribution* (the spending-of-savings years), share several similarities. They take place in similar time frames; each phase lasts between twenty-five and forty years (recall, however, that this is a recent occurrence; in past generations, the distribution phase represented only a decade, maybe two if the person lived a very long time). During both phases, foundational principles of investing are of critical importance. Concurrently, in both phases, market risk is an inevitability that must be managed.

A person spends their working years accumulating

resources that will be distributed during retirement. The money accumulated will serve as the basis for the person's retirement income for decades. We'll focus on this more over the next several pages on the *distribution* phase.

DISTRIBUTION IN DEPTH

Financially speaking, the place where a person can make the single greatest impact on their retirement is in exactly how they plan to turn their accumulated resources, their savings, into income for the rest of their lives. Other forms of income, like social security and pensions, also come into play; however, we know that where you can have the most ability to impact your retirement income, for good or bad, is in the proper management and distribution of your accumulated savings.

In simple terms, planning income for the distribution phase involves deciding exactly how to create a regular income out of a retiree's accumulated investments.

For many retirees, the distribution phase represents the first time in their lives that their investments and their income are tightly intertwined. Throughout the accumulation phase, a person's investments are largely separate; they likely have a 401(k) that remains untouched, and they may have non-retirement investments. Their *income*, though, is totally separate from those entities; it's the steady check deposited into their bank account to be used in the *now*, whereas investments are money planned for the future.

In the distribution phase of a person's life, suddenly their investments *are* their income; or, at the very least, those investments constitute a component of their monthly or annual income. In order to produce a consistent and dependable income that can grow to offset inflation, one must marry their investment and income strategies in such a way that they are prepared for the shorter-term risks (market and withdrawal) and longer-term risks (inflation, longevity, tax) a retiree will face. Having a plan in place in order to manage these risks is so important to a retiree's future income that we have dedicated an entire chapter to it later in the book.

Another key impact on the distribution phase is the financial concerns that are unique to people of retirement age, primarily the rising costs of healthcare. A distribution plan that does not adequately take these costs, which increase with age and can be unpredictable, into account will create a retirement in which carefully won confidence is lost when things go wrong.

Without a plan, the distribution phase can quickly go wrong. Mistakes made early on compound as the margin for error compresses over time. More than anything, it's important for a retiree to carefully and thoroughly plan for the distribution phase of their life.

We worked with a couple years ago who made several common errors in the time leading up to their retirement. At first glance, they seemed reasonably well-prepared for their retirement, with a paid-off house, social security, and several million dollars. The problem, we discovered, was that on the advice of their broker, they had recently moved their money into a more conservative portfolio, from which the expected rate of return has little chance of keeping up with normal rates of inflation.

Inflation is like carbon monoxide. You can't see it, taste it, or smell it, but it'll kill you—or, metaphorically speaking, compromise your financial security, if not properly planned for.

As a result of the rise of inflation, these clients had dipped into their principal again and again over the decades just to keep pace with the rising cost of living. By the time we met them, they were in their late seventies. At that point in a person's life, it's difficult to even consider a different approach to their investment and income strategy; they're locked into a dangerous pattern.

PULLING THE PIECES TOGETHER

This book will focus on the distribution phase and all the most impactful factors that go into successfully planning the distribution phase of a retiree's life. We'll dive into subjects like how inflation plays into the equation, when to apply for social security, how to budget and set income goals, how to invest well and intentionally, and how to manage market risk. Our intention is to create confidence through knowledge.

Once the foundational principles of this crucial time are understood, and the biggest mistakes to be made are identified and avoided, an actionable, simple plan for resource distribution in retirement will hopefully appear much more accomplishable than perhaps you've previously been led to believe.

A SUCCESSFUL RETIREMENT STARTS WITH A PLAN

The act of constructing a sound retirement income plan requires an investment of time and money on both sides: that of the financial advisor, and that of the retiree. It requires a commitment to educating oneself on the basics of investment and income planning, and to doing the work of creating and sticking to a plan. This investment of time and energy will pay dividends for years to come.

Recently, a prospective client made clear to us that he

simply wanted the work to be done for him and that educating himself wasn't high on his priority list.

"I don't want to be educated," he told us. "I want you to tell me what to do. You're the experts, right?"

"We are," I said. "But with all due respect, Louis, our process is to lead with education in order to help our clients make informed decisions. What we have found over the years is that when a client plays a role in the decision regarding planning and strategies, they become intellectually and, more importantly, emotionally committed to the plan. And as a result of that commitment, they typically experience more successful outcomes."

We didn't take him on as a client because we knew that a retiree who can't even commit to *creating* a plan likely won't be able to follow one once he's retired.

By contrast, we've seen hundreds of clients move from a mindset of anxiety and immobility to one of confidence, education, and commitment simply by doing the work to create their retirement plan. Creating the plan is simple, but not easy. It requires work, discipline, and trust in the process.

The benefit of a well-planned retirement, though, speaks for itself. If you're entering the transition to your retirement, you're moving into a period of tremendous emotional transition, as well as financial flux and sometimes physical upheaval. The plan you set now will act as a guide and as reassurance throughout, and ensure that, on the other side, you're able to enjoy what you've been looking forward to: freedom.

CHAPTER TWO

———

VISUALIZE YOUR FUTURE WITH CLEAR GOALS

"When it comes to retirement planning, I'm just hoping it all works out."

This statement was made to us recently by a client, and it reflects so much of the widespread mindset we see in people facing retirement.

The woman who stated this actually repeated it three times during our meeting with her: "I'm just hoping for the best." She had no concrete goals whatsoever; she knew that retirement had to happen at some point, but she felt stalled by fear and lack of knowledge, and had decided to forgo doing any real planning and instead opted for what we call the "hopeium" strategy. In doing so, she was unprepared for the road ahead.

She had, in essence, decided to stick her head in the sand and avoid reality.

In reality, planning for retirement is never as daunting as it looks. But when someone facing an uncertain future sticks their head in the sand and avoids that uncertainty, they are *making it harder to achieve* success. Avoidance never solves anything, and while a problem is being avoided, it's only growing larger; the stakes grow higher, and the time in which the problem can be addressed effectively shrinks. In committing to education and planning, you may not always get the answer you're looking for, but there is nearly always a way to reach the goals you set if you remain adaptable and willing to learn.

WHAT WILL RETIREMENT LOOK LIKE?

Retirement can often seem like an unknown frontier to those nearing it. What will it look like not to go to work every day? What will it be like to rely not on a regular paycheck, but on a carefully crafted retirement income strategy? What about all the extra time—what will fill the days?

THE FOUR FREEDOMS

During their working decades, most people sacrifice much of their own desires for the needs of their spouses, their children, and their jobs or businesses. Once they begin nearing retirement, however, it begins to dawn on a retiree that they'll have the energy to focus on the things they want to do, the person they want to be, and the influence they hope to have on the world around them.

Author and founder of Strategic Coach Dan Sullivan identified the reason most entrepreneurs are motivated to set out on their own and create a living without any guarantee of success. The reason isn't making a name for themselves, or even building wealth; the reason is *freedom*. Specifically, there are four freedoms that inspire most entrepreneurs, and we believe soon-to-be and recent retirees: freedom of time, money, purpose, and relationship.[1]

Freedom of Time

Working a nine-to-five job involves just that: dedicating yourself to something other than your own desires for eight hours a day, five days a week. Once you've retired, however, you've suddenly gained forty plus hours a week; you can focus those hours on whatever you want. For

---

1 Dan Sullivan, *Strategic Coach*. http://blog.strategiccoach.com/
4-freedoms-motivate-successful-entrepreneurs/

the typical retiree, this is an incredible freedom; they're able to devote themselves to passions that simply took a backseat to family and career obligations during their working years.

Freedom of Money

Having a solid retirement income plan doesn't completely free you from monetary concerns; after all, committing to the plan is a daily necessity, and sometimes the plan involves being conscious and careful with financial resources in order to meet long-term goals. But in general, the typical retiree enjoys a type of monetary freedom that is deeply rewarding: they are free from the worry that they won't have enough money to live on, or that something will happen to make their flow of income cease. They have a plan, and they're confident that they'll be able to accomplish their future goals.

Freedom of Purpose

Although the places people tend to find purpose differ wildly between individuals, finding purpose in an activity or organization often inspires a higher level of personal fulfillment than one's career. When a person is required to work for their paycheck forty hours a week, their ability to commit to fulfilling activities takes a backseat. Once retired, however, many people find themselves free to pursue those activities, and to build fulfillment and contentment that extends far beyond money.

Freedom of Relationship

During your career, you're often confined to spending time with people chosen for the job, not people you've chosen to build relationships with. It seems obvious, but the impact of being free to choose who you spend time with and how you build and foster relationships in retirement has an incredible impact on the retiree's state of mind and general happiness.

When it comes to retirement, your first step in planning should be to consider the four freedoms, and envision what your ideal exercise of these freedoms might look like.

YOUR RETIREMENT, YOUR GOALS

Just "hoping for the best" isn't a plan. Neither is simply planning *not* to retire. After all, sooner or later in their lives, everyone will need to stop working, and when that time comes, they'll need money put aside to cover their basic needs, at the very least.

Yogi Berra, the baseball player, famously said, "You've got to be very careful if you don't know where you're going, because you might not get there."

The earlier you plan, the more runway you give yourself later on. Planning begins with deciding what you *want* out of your retirement—it begins with setting goals.

In popular culture and business alike, there's a lot of talk about setting goals. However, in practice, less than 80 percent of the population has written goals in any area of their life. This is particularly true when it comes to constructive retirement goals.

People fail to set retirement goals as a direct result of their lack of confidence or knowledge regarding personal finance. This is not unusual; in fact, we see it all the time. Lack of a clear understanding around where retirement income will come from or how much will be available means they don't have the baseline necessary to even begin thinking about realistic retirement goals. They lack a clear vision of what life will look like once they leave the workforce.

Goal-setting and budgeting serve as the foundation of a well-developed plan. A realistic sense of the retirement income you need provides the information necessary to establish appropriate goals and alleviates the fear of the unknown.

THE FIRST PRIORITY

Ask any soon-to-be retiree what their number one goal for retirement is, and you're likely to get a slightly different answer each time; however, you'll notice a pattern if you ask the question of enough people.

Most retirees' number one goal for retirement is to maintain their lifestyle. No one wants to move backward; not only would it require changing, sometimes in drastic ways, the way one lives, it also goes against our deeply ingrained American cultural urge to keep improving, keep leveling up. People want to continue to be able to live the way they're accustomed to, and they want to be able to maintain their dignity and independence. At the bare minimum, they don't want to become a burden to their families.

With diligent planning, and if needed, a plan to course-correct, maintaining one's lifestyle should be clearly within a retiree's grasp. However, a common problem among those planning for retirement is that lifestyle maintenance is where their goal-setting stops. A goal that large in scope and non-specific in execution isn't going to lead to a well-made plan.

Organized goal-setting is not an optional part of retirement income planning. It is essential. Without clearly defined goals, your income plan is not grounded in reality. This results in the need for course-correction either during retirement or in the years immediately leading up to it. Often, such corrections can be quite significant.

VISUALIZING RETIREMENT

Life doesn't end with retirement. In fact, in many ways, retirement represents a new beginning. With retirement comes time, freedom, and flexibility that are not available to many during their working years. This worksheet is designed to help you think beyond your current situation and begin to visualize where you want to focus your attention in your retirement years. What areas of life are not currently receiving focus and attention? How will you be able to redistribute that attention during your retirement years? This worksheet will serve as the first step in establishing goals that will set you up for a fulfilling retirement.

Access a downloadable version here:

http://www.questcapitalmanagement.com/downloadable-files

Circle of Life Worksheet

Directions:

This exercise will help you to assess your growth and development in each Facet of Life. It will also help you to evaluate the degree of balance and level of life satisfaction you are now experiencing.

1. Place a dot on each spoke that indicates your level of satisfaction in that particular Facet of Life. Use a scale of 0 to 10, with 0 at the hub and 10 at the rim. A 0 indicates no satisfaction, and a 10 indicates the highest degree of satisfaction.

2. Now draw a line to connect the dots and create your life wheel.

3. Examine: is your life wheel round, or does it show flat spots? Is it deflated or is it full? What does this exercise tell you about your life? Is your life balanced? Are there areas of your life that need attention? In what facets would you like to experience more satisfaction?

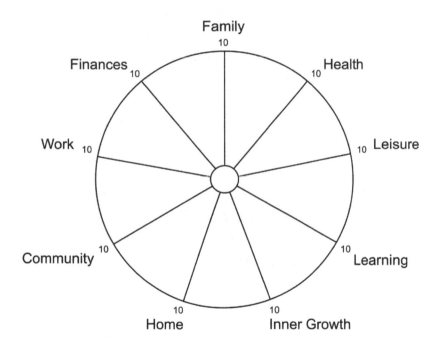

Vague goals are not any more helpful than *no* goals. In fact, nebulous goals can be even more detrimental than a lack of goals altogether because they provide people with the illusion that they have a working plan. "I want to retire by the time I'm sixty-two" is a goal, but it isn't concrete enough to provide the structure for realistic retirement planning. It leaves far too much room for error.

UNDERSTANDING WHAT YOU'LL NEED

It's rare for us to meet a new client who has already accurately assessed what they currently spend and has undergone a thoughtful review of what future spending will look like. Doing a budget sheet is an eye-opening experience for many; in addition, rarely have they given further thought to how the costs of their goods and services will increase through the years. As a result, a common error of retirees is to underestimate how much money they'll need in retirement.

"Needs" are relative, but everyone begins with the same basic set of needs: housing, food, transportation, and health care. These essential living expenses are the first thing that must be planned in any retirement budget.

Once those needs are budgeted, a higher order of needs can be considered. These needs include feeling independent, maintaining one's lifestyle, feeling fulfilled, and pursuing passions. These aspects of retirement are deeply important, but the monetary cost inherent in fulfilling these needs can easily be underestimated by retirees.

Prioritizing your goals is crucial to making sure you're creating goals that can be met.

CREATING CONSTRUCTIVE GOALS

Constructive goals are specific and realistic. We recently met with a client of ours to help him clarify, prioritize, and assign costs to his important retirement goals. Through some discussion and with the help of the worksheets in this chapter, he was able to articulate the following: "I'm fifty-eight right now and want to retire by the time I'm sixty-two. I have calculated that I'll need an income of $85,000 per year after taxes to maintain my current lifestyle. I would also like to travel while I am still healthy, so I'll budget in an additional $10,000 per year for ten years to account for travel. I have two children whom I would like to gift $25,000 each. If I can't achieve these goals at sixty-two, I'm willing to work longer in order to accomplish them."

After running the numbers, it became clear that, while all of this client's goals would be possible were he to retire at age sixty-six, it would not possible at sixty-two. Our client had the option to either pare down or omit some of his goals, or to continue working for an additional four years, which would provide him with the best chance of the retirement he envisioned. He ultimately prioritized his specific goals, making the decision to continue to work until age sixty-six, with the knowledge that four additional years in the workforce would earn him a retirement that looks the way he wants it to.

Of course, not everyone will have the option to work for an extended amount of time for any number of reasons. It might be health-related, or it could be that a job simply disappears in a changing economy. However, establishing priorities and working through what different scenarios will realistically look like empowers retirees. It allows them to make decisions with a clear understanding of how they will impact their future income, lifestyle, and flexibility.

Elements of an Effective Goal

Notice that within our client's example goal, he included several important factors: the annual income necessary to maintain his current lifestyle, additional annual income for visionary pursuits, and significant one-time expenses. These represent several important elements that should be included in every constructive goal:

- They should be prioritized
- Frequency of expenditures
- Specific timeline
- Specific dollar amounts
- A back-up plan

Another critical component of our client's goal is that he included goals that were immediate (cost of lifestyle maintenance), short- to mid-term (travel), and long-term (gifting children with $25,000). Increasingly, retirement can represent a large portion of your life. Short-sighted visioning and goal-setting may very well not account for the reality of retirement. It's important to set goals that extend beyond the short term.

SETTING GOALS FOR RETIREMENT

To serve as an effective tool, this worksheet requires careful contemplation and visualization about the day-to-day realities of retired life. As you track your goals, consider the ways in which your daily life will be different in retirement than it is today, and how your life, needs, and preferences will likely evolve over the next couple of decades.

Access a downloadable version here:

http://www.questcapitalmanagement.com/downloadable-files

Goal Clarifying Worksheet

Directions:

1. Identify your most important life goals and list them in the appropriate category below.

2. Next, write a few words (such as "increase security", "strengthen family ties", "have fun", "stretch my comfort zones") to describe your reason for each goal.

3. Now estimate the financial investment required to achieve each goal. A "guesstimate" is fine; these figures can always be refined as you gather more information. In addition, consider the investment of time, energy, and other resources that will be needed.

4. After you have completed your lists, assign a priority status of A, B, or C to each goal.

Immediate Goals and Priorities

Life Goal	Reason	Investment	Priority

Short-Term to Mid-Term Goals and Priorities (1 to 5 years)

Life Goal	Reason	Investment	Priority

Long-Term Goals and Priorities (5 years or longer)

Life Goal	Reason	Investment	Priority

YOUR RETIREMENT FOUNDATION

Recently, we worked with a client who was very resistant to setting retirement goals. In the course of our conversation, it became clear that she was afraid she didn't have enough money to retire. Her solution was to put off thinking about retirement at all and, instead, bury herself in continuing to work.

We showed this client that pragmatically working through the budgeting and goal-setting process would likely increase their feelings of control, clarity, direction, and confidence. In the worst-case scenario, the process would provide her with an understanding of what to realistically expect in retirement, alleviating her of the burden of imagining a future that would never come to fruition.

Running through the process with this client in black-and-white terms demonstrated that, not only did she have enough money to retire, but she could retire as early as she felt comfortable. Seeing her goals on paper made retirement real for our client and, within a year, she was happily retired. Not only was she meeting her basic needs, but she also recently closed on a beautiful vacation property in South Carolina while remaining well within her retirement budget.

The retirement income planning process can be complex. There's no way around that fact. You'll need to think through an appropriate investment strategy; you'll need to plan for many different types of risk; you'll need to incorporate an effective plan for taxes; and you'll need to think about how to maximize your guaranteed sources of income, like social security or a pension. At the most basic level, you'll need to understand where your retirement income will come from, and when and how you will best generate a growing stream of income for the rest of your life.

Even the most successful people in the world usually didn't go to school for *personal* finance. This isn't common knowledge, and that's partly why it can seem so overwhelming. But the most successful retirees are those who are open to the idea that they don't know everything, and seek help from qualified experts—legal, accounting, financial, insurance, and more—to help develop an overall retirement plan.

When it comes to retirement planning, you only have one shot. This is the most important thing to remember about setting goals and budgeting to meet those goals. By default, those entering retirement and planning for the next thirty or forty years of generating income have never created such a plan before. After all, no one plans for retirement twice! It's done once, and it *must* be done well if retirement is to be successful. Furthermore, it's a near guarantee that retirement plans will go wrong if the planning doesn't start out right.

Starting out right is entirely dependent on having a clear understanding of one's needs in retirement, and setting clear goals to form the foundation of a successful retirement that allows you to maintain the life you've built.

CHAPTER THREE

SOCIAL SECURITY: WHERE IT FITS AND WHAT YOU CAN EXPECT

Social security will represent several hundred thousand dollars of income over the course of one's retirement. Moreover, it has the comparative benefit of being inflation-adjusted, which is of enormous value in planning income that will need to last for, potentially, decades. As such, one of the most critical decisions in any retirement income plan is determining the point at which social security benefits should be claimed.

It's a decision that, once made, for the most part, is irreversible—so, you want to get it right. Fortunately, with some basic education as to how social security will affect your income throughout retirement, it's a decision that can be made with confidence. This book isn't meant as a comprehensive breakdown of the mechanics of social security. However, what we aim to provide is a basic set of knowledge that will serve any retiree in considering their social security claiming strategy. It's a very important decision that we believe should be made in the context of your overall retirement income plan.

When social security was established in 1935, the system was created based on an assumption that for every thirty-seven active workers contributing to the fund, one retiree could be supported. This coincided with a historical life expectancy of sixty-one, and an average retirement age of sixty-five—the juxtaposition of which suggests that social security was not anticipated to be claimed by each and every worker who contributed during their career.

Today, the landscape is vastly different. The ratio of participants to beneficiaries is not thirty-seven to one, but *three* to one. And, while the average retirement age of sixty-five has remained more or less constant, life expectancy in America is now eighty-three.

This marked shift in the basic math at the foundation of social security has contributed to a preponderance of alarmism and myths surrounding the fund, and has led to many retirees not taking social security as seriously as they should. We've heard people express to us, "Well, I have social security, but it won't be very much," or even, "by the time I retire, social security may not be there."

These fears are common but unfounded. Social security will absolutely be an important part of any retiree's income plan. In fact, for many retirees, it's the second biggest decision they will make in planning their retirement. To dismiss its importance, or even discount it as a possibility—thereby neglecting the planning of that future income—would be to the detriment of one's retirement success.

SOCIAL SECURITY: REALITY VS. MYTH

As mentioned previously, your social security benefit is inflation-adjusted, or in Social-Security-speak, it has a Cost of Living Adjustment (COLA).

This is a much heftier benefit than it initially appears—after all, 2.6 percent doesn't *seem* like all that much, but over the course of more than two decades, it represents a significant sum.

Here's what inflation-adjusted income might look like in practice. Let's say a retiree receives $2,000 per month in social security income. But, since that benefit will adjust for inflation, it will grow on average 2.6 percent per year; over a thirty-year period of time, that $2,000 per month will amount to approximately $1.1 million in social security benefits.

It's important to look at social security, then, on the scale of a *lifetime* benefit, as well as a monthly benefit. Only by viewing it as part of a long-term strategy can the true impact of social security be seen clearly.

Many people err by making social security decisions in a vacuum, rather than viewing them in the context of a holistic, highly strategized retirement income plan. There also exists a pervasive pattern of basing social security decisions on preconceived—and, often, erroneous—notions. These notions might be inherited from our parents, rooted in a general lack of education about personal finance, or derived from the media. Put simply, many people we meet have formed misconceptions about social security that have caused them to underestimate its weight in their retirement plan.

Wherever they may stem from, these misconceptions often serve as the basis for crucial financial decisions. They are at the root of hastily made decisions that are not grounded in fact. Worst of all, these decisions potentially come at the cost of a significant financial loss of potential retirement income, and as we discuss later in the chapter, where there is a spouse to consider, could significantly impact the surviving spouse's financial well-being.

MYTH #1: PERCENTAGE OF RETIREMENT INCOME

When asked, most people believe that social security will account for 35 percent of their retirement income; in reality, studies show that social security represents, on average, 62 percent of a retiree's income in retirement. Many retirees are far more dependent on their social security benefits than they had anticipated. This dependence on social security is based on three primary factors:

1. If the retiree did not save enough for retirement (or, conversely, they over-spent throughout their accumulation years). As a result, social security will be a much larger component of their income.

2. If the retiree failed to realistically plan for the cost of retirement, which results in underestimating the amount of income they will need throughout their retirement years. Again, as a result, social security becomes a higher percentage of a retiree's income.

3. If the retiree did not do the work to create a long-term plan for converting savings to income, they are much more likely to need to rely more heavily on social security for income than they had anticipated. In other words, if they did not develop a solid investment strategy for producing a growing stream of income for life. and subsequently exposed their nest egg to the five risks a retirement portfolio will face.

The bottom line is that social security will represent a lot of money to the average retiree. Its importance can't be dismissed, and any decisions about social security should be made with the full weight of careful and well-informed consideration.

MYTH #2: SOCIAL SECURITY WILL DISAPPEAR

Despite what the media and conventional wisdom might lead you to believe, social security is not going anywhere. According to the 2016 Social Security Trustee's Report, social security is 100 percent funded through the year 2033. For the years 2034 through 2090, between 74 and 79 percent of promised benefits are funded.

In the sixteen years between now and 2034, it is highly possible that legislation will bridge this gap to bring the social security funding percentage back up to 100 percent. All of this means that if you are reading this book, you are assured to receive, at the very least, the vast majority of your social security benefits.

The alleged bankruptcy of social security makes compelling copy for the media, but it is simply not true. This widespread fallacy is the source of a lot of financial anxiety, which dictates many people's social security decisions. Few good decisions, financial or otherwise, have ever been born of anxiety.

The worst decision that could arise from this particular myth is claiming social security too early. The thinking goes, "Social security is going to disappear, so I'd better claim it as soon as I'm able to get my share!"

Claiming too early is an all-too-common mistake, and the

potential loss to the retiree is enormous over the course of their retirement. There is strategy involved in claiming social security, and to make a good decision that sets up a retiree for success, that strategy should be based on facts, not conjecture or conventional wisdom.

SOCIAL SECURITY CLAIMING CONSIDERATIONS
LIFETIME EARNINGS

The total amount of a retiree's social security benefit is dependent upon two primary factors: lifetime earnings, and the age at which an applicant chooses to begin receiving their benefit.

Determining your social security benefit amount is as simple as logging onto the Social Security Administration website at www.ssa.gov and establishing online access.

The total amount of social security benefit to be received is calculated based on the average of the highest thirty-five years' worth of workforce earnings. Any years during which no income was earned for any reason will be listed as a zero, and when included in an average, these zero sums can significantly and negatively impact your social security benefit amount.

APPLICATION TIMEFRAME

Social security benefits can be accessed as early as age sixty-two. However, it's important to note that a significant and irrevocable financial penalty is assessed to those who apply before full retirement age. This penalty can represent a reduction of anywhere from 25 to 30 percent of your social security benefit, and will remain in effect for the remainder of your lifetime.

The full retirement age is currently sixty-six years and two months; it will gradually rise to age sixty-seven for those born in 1960 or later. Those who apply for benefits between full retirement age up to the age of seventy will earn what SS calls delayed credits, which is a lifetime premium (in other words, they will maximize their potential benefits). After the age of seventy, there is no further benefit to waiting to claim.

Every extra year that a person waits to claim social security benefits between the ages of sixty-two and full retirement age increases their social security benefit by an average of 5 percent. This represents a 5 percent growth on guaranteed, inflation-adjusted income.

Social security benefits will increase by 8 percent, inflation-adjusted, per year for every year they remain unclaimed between the ages of full retirement and seventy. This means that the difference between claiming social security at sixty-six and seventy represents an approximate 32 percent increase of the total monthly benefit, thereby increasing your overall lifetime earnings.

As a result, waiting to claim your social security benefit until the age of seventy pays off significantly. For example, a retiree who will earn $1,950 per month by claiming his retirement benefit at age sixty-two will increase his benefit amount to $2,600 by claiming at age sixty-six. This amount balloons to $4,212 per month by waiting until age seventy. This final amount is more than double what the retiree would receive were he to claim his benefits eight years earlier at age sixty-two.

HEALTH AND FAMILY

There are a few legitimate reasons for opting to claim social security benefits at an earlier age. Factors that may impact this decision include personal health, family history, and marital status.

Those who are single, in poor health, or who have a family history of early death may be wise to claim their benefits closer to age sixty-two. Determining factors in this scenario include a lower life expectancy and the fact that spousal longevity is not a consideration.

However, a person who is healthy, has a family history of

long life expectancy, and has a spouse's lifetime to consider should generally opt to delay for as long as possible, even though it may mean deciding to work a little longer or temporarily over-withdrawing from an IRA or investment account to bridge the income gap.

SPOUSAL PLANNING

Spousal retirement planning is slightly more complex for the simple reason that two lifetimes, not one, must be considered. Many people we work with have not considered that, upon the death of one spouse, the surviving spouse will be left with only the higher social security benefit. They also haven't considered how important maximizing that remaining benefit will be to the surviving spouse's lifetime income.

With two lifetimes to consider, the likelihood of at least one spouse reaching the age of ninety or beyond increases significantly. In the event of a death, the surviving spouse will continue to receive only the higher benefit amount for the duration of their lifetime; therefore, generally speaking, the higher-earning spouse should delay claiming social security benefits for as long as possible in order to maximize income.

Here's a real-world example: A client of ours was determined to claim his social security benefits at age sixty-six.

When we asked him why, he said, "Well, in order to break even on what I contributed, I'd need to live to my mid-seventies. What if I don't live that long? I want to claim as soon as I can, so I can be sure to at least break even."

"Mark," we said, "Have you thought about how long Mary is going to live?"

He hadn't thought about his wife's life expectancy in the context of social security claiming. It simply hadn't occurred to him. And, when spousal life expectancy is factored into the decision, the concept of "breaking even" holds little weight at all.

We laid out the numbers for Mark, showing his benefit at age sixty-six and at age seventy. It turned out that the difference between claiming his social security benefits at sixty-six versus seventy would cost them a total of $350,000 over the combined lifetimes of him and his wife. In other words, if his wife outlived him, he'd be costing her over a quarter of a million dollars.

In our work as advisors, our aim is not to *persuade* anyone. Little of what we do is based on opinion; it's based on fact. And with Mark, when we laid out the facts for him, he didn't need any persuading at all. The flaw in his plan was obvious, and he adjusted his plan.

THE KEY TAKEAWAY

In the context of your overall retirement planning, your social security decision is the second most important decision you'll make. It's not a decision to be made lightly, and if in reading this chapter, you've recognized that you share any of the misconceptions we outlined, do yourself the service of researching the subject further. The only good decision you can make on social security will be one born of education and facts and tied to your personal circumstances.

When you've done the work to learn about your social security position and options, you'll undoubtedly still have questions. At that point, we recommend seeking the advice of a qualified social security expert. The Social Security Administration does provide basic Q&A and advice, but their motivation will not be to help you maximize your benefit—they serve the fund, not you. Seek a dedicated professional who will help you navigate the complexity of social security, and who will be motivated to serve you best and who will explain your options to maximize your social security benefits.

Most of all, take social security seriously! It's a subject that is so often dismissed in conversations about retirement planning, but it represents a significant sum of money no matter where your net worth currently stands. Include it in your retirement planning considerations with the same weight you give to planning the rest of your income streams. Once you've made a good decision, you can relax; it's behind you, and you can simply enjoy the benefit.

RECAP: KEY POINTS FOR YOUR SOCIAL SECURITY DECISION

Pull down your most recent social security statement from www. ssa.gov and become familiar with it. Build a solid understanding of the numbers behind a variety of social security decisions, such as the difference in lifetime benefits if you claim at age sixty-two versus age sixty-seven, or even beyond.

Make a list of all other sources of guaranteed retirement income—such as a pension—and calculate how much of your guaranteed retirement income will be represented by your social security benefits.

Take your marital and health statuses into account. Whether you're married or single, and whether you're healthy or require medical aid, will impact your decision on when to begin claiming social security benefits.

Don't make your social security decision in a vacuum. Consider it as part of an overall retirement income and investment plan. Research all of your options so that you can understand how social security will affect your retirement income plan long-term.

Social security is complex—there's no putting that lightly. There are many claiming strategies out there that you may run across in your research, and it can be confusing to figure out which strategy to take. We ourselves—experts in our industry—routinely seek outside advice from dedicated social security experts, because the subject is so complex. We recommend that you do the same before any decision is set in stone.

Part Two

PRACTICAL RETIREMENT INCOME PLANNING

For decades, conventional wisdom has used a common analogy to describe retirement planning: they visualize the process as a three-legged stool. Each leg of the stool represents the three sources of income a retiree should plan. These three sources used to be social security, pension, and savings. However, due to the decline of pensions as an expected form of guaranteed income, we believe today's retiree should visualize a three-legged stool supported by income planning, investment planning, and tax planning.

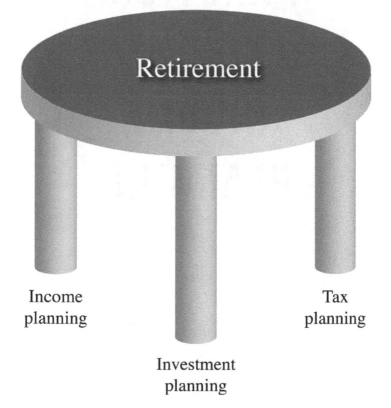

Income
planning

Tax
planning

Investment
planning

This visual better represents the reality faced by those entering retirement today. In order to produce a growing stream of income for upwards of three decades of retirement, and to meet their life goals, it is of paramount importance that a retiree carefully understands how interrelated these three areas become. How those investments are managed directly impacts the tax planning and income planning of the retiree.

In the last three chapters, we laid out the fundamental decisions, steps, and actions of retirement income planning, and explained the high-level concepts you must understand when developing a plan for converting your savings into income.

In these next three chapters, we'll dig deeper into the nuts and bolts of how to think about converting your savings to income. You'll get a clearer understanding of the immediate steps you can take to begin developing a customized strategy.

We'll focus on five core principles and disciplines that you will need to follow in order to become a successful retirement income investor, and as a result, create a growing stream of income for life:

1. Asset allocation
2. Investor behavior

3. Rebalancing
4. Diversification
5. Understanding and identifying risk

In the following chapters, we'll explain each of these principles in detail. We'll also help you get a sense of what kind of professional advice you should seek when you're ready to put your plan into action.

It's important that you understand as you read through these next chapters that none of the information within is based on our opinion or popular wisdom. Everything we are about to walk you through is evidenced-based *fact* that is supported by decades of research and review conducted by academic and commercial institutions. Our intention is that the information we lay out for you in the next three chapters goes a long way to shut down the financial "noise" out there—the media, the well-intentioned relatives and friends, and possibly the financial professionals you may have encountered.

Put simply, what you're about to read is what *works*. Pay close attention.

CHAPTER FOUR

≡

INVESTMENT FUNDAMENTALS 101

"Human nature is a failed investor."

NICK MURRAY

The average investor makes predictable mistakes; from beginners just getting their feet wet with their first brokerage account, to those who feel comfortable trading their own accounts, the human emotion and psychology driving investor behavior lead to money lost on a consistent basis.

For a person in their accumulation phase, investment mistakes are simply that—mistakes, to be weathered and learned from. In their distribution phase, however, the same person doesn't have the same room for mistakes. The runway is much, much shorter. The cost of unnecessary mistakes is much higher. And the ability to correct down the line, change course and make up for lost ground, is curtailed.

Recently, we met with a man who was headed into retirement with $750,000 in his 401(k). However, this $750,000 was not, as it should have been, properly invested; the majority had been sitting static in a money market account for the past decade, with very little allocated to stocks and bonds.

We learned that he had, like so many others, reacted without forethought during the market crisis of 2008, and had exited the market with $520,000, just a portion of his portfolio. He had then been so paralyzed with fear of losing his money that he'd never figured out when to get back in.

This is a mistake we have seen more than once. People make rash decisions out of fear, a lack of education, and a lack of preparation and strategy. They find themselves totally ill-equipped to distinguish between risk and volatility. Had this man developed a well-thought-out investment strategy and consistently followed it, he could have potentially doubled his money in the subsequent ten years. Being subject to his own fear was all that prevented him from having significantly more money at retirement.

Another common mistake we see is under-diversifying. The best illustration of this phenomenon is a former client of ours, Ray. Ray initially engaged our services right after the Tech Wreck. He brought us a brokerage statement that showed, at its height, his portfolio of tech stocks had been worth around one million dollars. When we met him, it had plummeted to a little over $350,000.

Ray thought all along he'd been investing wisely, putting his money into well-known tech funds that capitalized on the enormous market opportunity of the 1990s. However, what he failed to realize, and what so many like him fail to realize, is that diversification is a huge component of successfully weathering extreme market events. The tech funds he'd invested in were all, essentially, holding the same stocks. Without realizing it, he was woefully under-diversified. When the Tech Wreck hit, his portfolio uniformly went down the drain.

He knew he'd made a rather large mistake, and he was scared. He had no idea how he was going to maintain his lifestyle, let alone have a successful retirement. Now, eighteen years later, Ray is still working, not feeling secure or confident in being able to maintain the life he and his family were accustomed to if he retired.

Mistakes like these aren't one-offs; we have seen several over the years. They occur because people lack the education they need to make informed decisions on how to appropriately invest their money, and they have not thought through, or have failed to understand, the risk associated with their portfolios. They fail to account for unpredictability, and when things go wrong, they panic.

Even putting aside extreme cases like Ray's, countless studies show that the average investor makes smaller versions of these mistakes and more, and those mistakes add up to between 3 and 4 percent per year.[2] Three percent doesn't seem like much, but over the course of a multi-decade retirement, 3 percent can add up to a significant amount. Consider the investor with a $1 million portfolio. If that investor makes the common mistakes that are often made, they may be costing themselves $30,000 or more per year! The popular financial media sends the message to its viewership that *anyone* can be a successful investor if they simply choose the right stocks, get in and out of the market at the correct time, and pay little to no fees for the management of their portfolio. In reality, it's been proven over and over again that that strategy can be a recipe for disaster. When an investor puts their primary focus into market timing and selection and seeks no professional help, they're typically making disconnected, ad-hoc decisions that aren't part of a larger plan. They're making decisions by default, rather than by design. These decisions are reactive, rather than proactive.

2   Dalbar Study 2017, https://www.dalbar.com/QAIB/Index

For the typical baby boomer who is headed into retirement without a pension, and with solely the safety net of social security and the accumulated wealth of their assets, reactive, unplanned investor behavior focused on timing and selection may very well *hinder* their retirement income.

It's important to understand that the vast majority of popular, of-the-moment investment suggestions touted by the media is usually the *wrong* advice to follow. Mistakes made as a result of unwise investor behavior become harder and harder to correct as time goes on.

Informed decisions, decisions based on fact, research, and well-formulated strategy, are what yield the result you as a retiree are looking for: a confident and smooth retirement, where you get to maintain your lifestyle, meet your goals, and live the four freedoms to their fullest extent.

WHAT DRIVES INVESTOR RESULTS (IT'S NOT WHAT YOU THINK!)

When most people think of success in wealth-building through investments, their minds flash to famous stories of investors picking one great stock before it was a winner, then riding the wave as that stock's stratospheric rise carried them to riches. They become obsessed with the idea of researching stocks, picking just the right one, and trying to pinpoint the precise moment they should buy it.

In doing so, they disregard the principles proven and followed by successful investors. By far, the single most important discipline to follow is your decision around your asset allocation. Despite this, very few investors understand how their assets are allocated.

Asset allocation is making disciplined, well-educated decisions about what percentage of your assets you will divide between stocks, bonds, and cash. In fact, academic studies prove time and time again that this decision is what drives 94 percent of investor results. It is not an investor's ability to pick a winning stock, nor their talent for deciding when is a good time to get in or out of the market, that builds investor success, regardless of what the popular media promotes. Selling magazines with colorful headlines, or driving up television viewership, is often what determines the information being promoted, rather than the motivation to provide consumers with factual and useful data. Often this is because the facts that should be provided are not sexy. Making an asset allocation decision and then holding that decision steady through all market cycles and outside forces won't sell many magazines or airspace; it won't provide fodder for flashy headlines. But it is, in truth, the way to win this game.

In the end, it's the decision you make regarding your allocations of stocks, bonds, and cash that will have the biggest impact on your retirement income. Think about it like riding a bicycle: when you first began to learn how to ride, the most fundamental concept to master was simply how to remain upright—how to keep from tipping over and falling to the ground. Once you understood that feeling of balance, you were able to ride a bike for the rest of your life. On a balanced bicycle, you can take a journey and feel confident you'll arrive at your destination. The same is true with your asset allocation decision. Find the right percentage of stocks and bonds that will help you get to where you want to go, which is creating a growing stream of income for life that supports all of your important life goals. Then keep that percentage balance steady throughout your retirement journey, only revisiting your decision in conjunction with major life events rather than outside, ever-changing noise. Contrary to popular belief, timing and selection have little substantial impact on investment results.

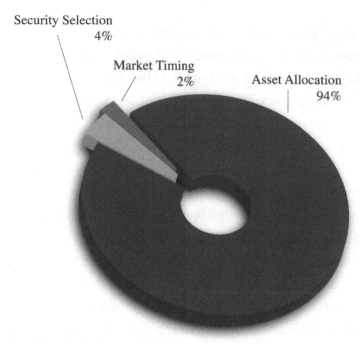

Security Selection
4%

Market Timing
2%

Asset Allocation
94%

Source: Brinson, Hood, and Beebower (BHB) (1986)

BEHAVIOR: INVESTORS ARE OFTEN THEIR OWN WORST ENEMY

Throughout your life before retirement, your income and your investments have been separate. For anyone in their working years, that's been the case. However, for anyone on the doorstep of retirement, or who is already in retirement, income and investments become very intertwined. It will become increasingly difficult to create a growing stream of income over time if your decision-making is fueled by emotion that is generated by the current headlines and pre-conceived notions.

Trying to manage behavior is a game not easily won. For

example, consider the self-help industry: billions of dollars per year are made selling books, videos, and gym memberships that are supposed to help you lose weight, stop smoking, or improve you in some other way. However, most people find that after these programs are purchased, they end up exactly where they started. The blame cannot be placed on the quality of self-help materials—the one constant is people's *behavior*, and in the end, people tend to be their own worst enemy. Sticking to a well-thought-out, evidenced-based investment and income strategy, ignoring the hype and fads of the moment, is by no means easy, especially when it pertains to your nest egg that you spent a lifetime saving. The consumer investor tends to do the wrong things at the wrong times, for the wrong reasons, usually costing themselves a lot of money over time.

2009 Market Performance & The #1 Factor in Client Results-Behavior

	S&P 500 Appreciation	# of Trading Days
Entire Year	27.8%	252
Feb. 9 - March 6	-21.4%	18
March 6 - April 24	26.8%	34
July 13 - Aug. 7	14.94%	200

Source: CFA Institute, *The New Wealth Management*, p 108

Let's take a look at both market timing and behavior by revisiting the year 2009. The chart *2009 Market Performance & the #1 Factor in Client Results-Behavior* tracks an extreme time in the markets, and it is not a question of *if* we will see this level of volatility again, but *when* we will see it again. It becomes very important, therefore, to understand that discipline is crucial if you hope to mitigate mistakes; investors who give in to reactive, emotional behavior will find their portfolios will suffer.

The year 2009 had 252 trading days in total, and between February 9th and March 6th, the S&P 500 fell 21.4 percent. To put this in context, this market tumble was on top of a steep fall at the end of 2008, representing an almost 50 percent decline in the S&P 500. At this point, it became clear that some investors either didn't have a plan, or failed to follow their plan, and gave in to fear and panic. Many made the decision to get out of the market, with the overriding thought, *let me preserve what I have left*. Of note, however, is what the next 34 trading days (between March 6th and April 24th) returned: a gain of 26.8 percent! You can be assured that those who sold around March 6th of that year were not confident enough to get back in the market within a few days, and thereby missed the market's overwhelmingly positive upturn. The chart further shows that from July 13th through August 7 the S&P 500 had an additional gain of 14.94 percent, with the entire year yielding an overall gain of 27.8 percent.

From the chart, you can draw two important conclusions. First, market volatility tends to come in short, sharp bursts, and patience and trust in a plan are required to weather those bursts. Second, trying to time the market is a nearly impossible feat. To time the market right, you would need to predict *exactly* the right time to get out— and then *exactly* the right time to get back in. The odds of you predicting these actions correctly and consistently are, to put it very simply, *not* in your favor. Making hasty, fear-based decisions such as those many made during the first few months of 2009 is often the result of lack of preparation—these investors were caught by surprise! They didn't really understand how much volatility their portfolio could face, and furthermore, this particular breath of volatility caught many seasoned investors and professionals by surprise as well. Knowing that you have a retirement income and investment plan in place that provides a strategy for insulating retirement income from being subject to market declines becomes imperative both analytically and emotionally. We will delve into this risk-mitigation strategy further in the next chapter.

EMOTIONS AND INVESTING: TIME TO BREAK THE CYCLE

Another excellent illustration of the impact of investor behavior is the historical performance of the S&P 500 compared to the average annual return of a typical equity (stock) fund investor over the course of a few decades. Between the years 1993 and 2015 the S&P 500, which isn't subject to the whims of human behavior, earned an average 8.19 percent return, while in the same time period, the typical equity fund investor averaged 4.67 percent. This represents a difference of 3.52 percent.

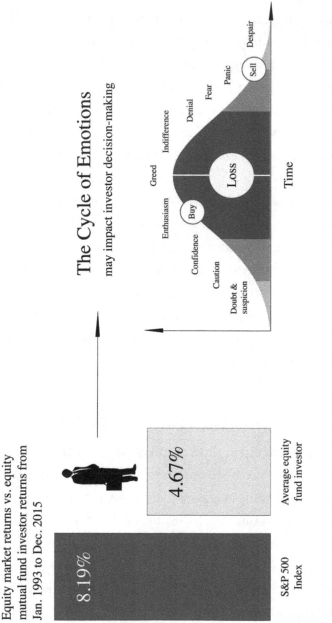

Average annual returns

Equity market returns vs. equity mutual fund investor returns from Jan. 1993 to Dec. 2015

8.19%

S&P 500
Index

4.67%

Average equity
fund investor

The Cycle of Emotions

may impact investor decision-making

Enthusiasm

Greed

Indifference

Confidence

Denial

Caution

Fear

Doubt &
suspicion

Panic

Buy

Sell

Despair

Loss

Time

Source: Dalbar, Inc., Quantitative Analysis of Investor Behavior, December 2015. The bar chart depicts the average annually compounded returns of equity indices vs. equity mutual fund investors based on the length of time shareholders actually remain invested in a fund and the historic performance of the fund's appropriate index. Past performance is no guarantee of future results. Investors cannot invest directly in an index.

Let's look at this cycle through the lens of a real investor. Dave, like many people, ended the year 2009 with a lot of doubt and distrust in the financial markets. He watched his accounts plummet almost 30 percent at the bottom of the decline. He entered 2010 with a lot of doubt and suspicion, "When will the next shoe drop?" Over the next three to five years, he began to cautiously re-enter the markets. It wasn't until the year 2017, however, when he felt truly enthusiastic about investing much more of his money in stock. It is understandable as to where the doubt and caution originated from; however, it did not serve his portfolio or retirement plans well. Dave's reality, like many, was that in the end he sold low and bought high. This goes a long way to explaining the difference in performance between the S&P 500 index and the average index investor. Why does this difference in return exist in study after study, year after year? Because investors are human beings, and whether we like to admit it or not, we tend to trade with emotion, and investor emotions run the gamut throughout any given market cycle.

Now let's take a look at how making decisions based on emotion or lack of education can affect a retiree's portfolio balance.

A TALE OF THREE INVESTORS

Here's what it would have looked like for three different

investors, each who invested $100,000 in the S&P 500 in January of 2007. The chart illustrates how their individual reactions to the extreme market volatility during the Great Recession of 2008 affected their balances as of 2016:

1. **Investor 1:** Stayed invested. They had a plan in place whereby they had considered all the applicable risks associated with a retirement income portfolio—which includes the reality that volatility will occur—and as a result, they were able to remain committed to their plan. By 2016, this investor had $174,812.

2. **Investor 2:** Sold in January of 2009 and got back in in January of 2010; then, in 2016, this investor had $113,895.

3. **Investor 3:** Sold in January of 2009 but did not reinvest due to fear. Then, in 2016, this investor had only $54,580 of their original $100k.

The Importance of Staying Invested

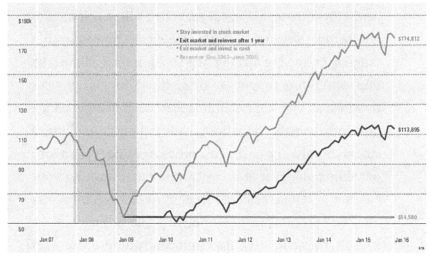

Source: © 2016 Morningstar

Investor 1 illustrates what having discipline and confidence in a well-thought-out plan look like when it comes to your investments. Later in this chapter and in subsequent chapters we will be laying out for you a simple yet effective plan to manage such market volatility.

REBALANCING: A THOUGHTFUL PROCESS OF WHEN TO BUY AND WHEN TO SELL

The next principle that needs to be understood and put into practice is rebalancing. This is an important risk and investment management discipline that works in concert with your asset allocation, and your diversification while providing a process for when to buy and when to sell. Remember the riding the bike analogy we spoke about earlier? The balance of your asset allocation that works for you because it will get you to where you want to go? Within the same analogy, *rebalancing* represents the ongoing method of making sure you don't fall off the bike. The term refers simply to a disciplined, regular process by which an investor maintains their desired asset allocation and diversification through the buying and selling of stocks, bonds, and cash. This process cannot be random or whimsical, as it is important for maintaining your balance and your selected level of risk. Many investors have no outlined process for buying and selling, and, as a result, they end up with a significantly different level of risk then they initially signed up for; they also may unwittingly suffer a lack of diversification. This breakdown of a portfolio's structure can ultimately compromise an investor's important life goals.

For example, say you made the decision in your income and investment strategy to maintain a portfolio of 60 percent stocks, 40 percent bonds. You happen to have an excellent year in the stock market with high returns. You end the year with more stock than when you began the year, and this means that your 60/40 allocation is now off. With an allocation of, let's say, 70 percent stocks, suddenly your portfolio has taken on more risk than you were willing to tolerate. It's time to regain your desired allocation by rebalancing back to your original targets.

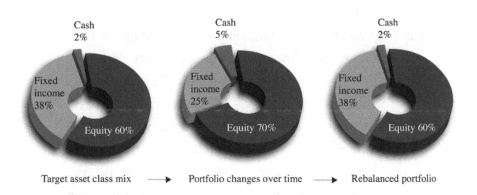

Cash
2%

Cash
5%

Cash
2%

Fixed
income
38%

Fixed
income
25%

Fixed
income
38%

Equity 60%

Equity 70%

Equity 60%

Target asset class mix ⟶ Portfolio changes over time ⟶ Rebalanced portfolio

Remember, your aim is to stay riding the bike, keeping the balance that works for you.

When a rebalance is triggered as a result of an inevitable drift due to market performance, a sell would be made on the better-performing investment. For example, during the first few months of 2009, we have already discussed how the S&P 500 (stocks) was down over 20 percent, on top of a nearly 30 percent decline in 2008. During this time, bonds were the better performing asset class. Due to the discipline of rebalancing, we were selling bonds and buying stock. Now, this can feel very counterintuitive! Stocks were declining rapidly, and we were buying them? Bonds were not nearly as volatile, and we were selling them? Let's look at another example where the process of selling the better performing asset class in order to rebalance may have felt counterintuitive. During 2017, the better performing asset class was stocks. In order to rebalance, some stock was sold, and the proceeds of that sale were used to buy the underperforming investment, which in 2017 was bonds. Often, we have found that it is natural to question, "Why are we selling stock when they're going up?" "Why would we buy bonds when they are not performing as well as stock?" The answer is because we have a process in place for when we buy and when we sell that is simply based on the numbers. Let's think about how powerful and beneficial this actually is: in the case of 2009, we sold bonds in order to rebalance back to our original target asset allocation and bought stock when they were very low. Selling high and buying low. That's a powerful advantage, especially if this discipline is performed as needed over a multi-decade retirement!

Being disciplined about rebalancing produces a thoughtful process of when you buy and when you sell, rather than a reactionary impulse to buy or sell, which the data and our experience tells us will lead to better results over time.

DIVERSIFICATION—THE INVESTOR'S EQUIVALENT TO BAKING A PIE

At a high level, diversification is the most easily understood of all of the basic investment principles. However, there's a caveat to that statement: diversification is also the most often *violated* of those principles.

The best illustration we use for the principles of diversification is a food metaphor. Think back to when you were a kid, to your favorite holiday. More than likely, your mother or father prepared some kind of special dessert to mark the occasion. For the sake of this example, let's say it was pignoli cookies.

Think of how much you loved those cookies, and how unique they were to the entire experience of your favorite holiday. The smell, the taste, and the texture were exactly as you expected—and that's why you remember them so well and so fondly.

Why, though, were those cookies so perfectly consistent year after year? It was because they were made with the same ingredients and a precisely followed recipe.

The same is true of a properly diversified investment portfolio. There are generally eleven main building blocks or asset classes that represent the ingredients of your portfolio. There are US Large Cap Stock, Small Cap Stock, and Mid Cap Stock, International, Emerging Markets, Real Estate, and more. You put those ingredients together using a thoughtful framework. The framework may call for different amounts of each ingredient—depending upon many factors, including but not limited to: personal circumstances, general economic conditions, interest rates, and domestic and international events. Having too much of one ingredient, too little of another, or leaving one out altogether, can ultimately compromise your recipe.

No matter how much or how little risk you're willing to take on as an investor, it is crucial to have a properly diversified portfolio. Recall our client Ray, who was under-diversified, and as a result, lost three-quarters of his nest egg in the Tech Wreck—you don't want that to be your story.

When an investor's portfolio is properly diversified, we can pretty much count on two things: the investor will never make a killing, but crucially, such a portfolio is never going to *get killed*. When it comes to your retirement income, diversifying your portfolio properly is the key to smoothing out your ride.

DIVERSIFICATION: INVESTOR BEHAVIOR REVISITED

Investors hurt themselves chasing after investments they feel—or have heard—are doing particularly well in a given year. It is not uncommon, as we mentioned earlier, for people to be insufficiently diversified. Without a plan and a process for when they buy and sell, they can disrupt the framework of a diversified portfolio. Often this disruption occurs when investors chase last year's winners with the expectation that the winning streak will continue. What is fact, however, is that there is little consistency from year to year in what investments will be the market leaders or losers, and even less predictability.

To illustrate this, let's take a look back to the year 1999. In that year, Emerging Markets (one of your portfolio's eleven asset classes) returned an incredible 66.4 percent! Now let's take a look at that same investment the following year. In the year 2000—Emerging Markets returned a *negative* 30.6 percent! On the flip side, yesterday's loser may also become tomorrow's winner; for example, US REITs (another asset class) in the year 1999 had a negative 4.6 percent return; however, in the following year, US REITs returned a gain of 26.4 percent.

What we can tell you is that when a particular investment asset class performs well, it creates a buzz. There can be a lot of press coverage and talk around the water cooler in companies around the nation, leading many investors to move money from lower performing investments into last year's winning investment. These investors have now sold low and bought high, and are most likely to be disappointed the following year. They have also, by chasing returns, disrupted their thoughtfully crafted framework of diversification.

Simply put, we diversify because we will never know from year to year which investments will be the winners and which will be the losers.

Owning a thoughtful "recipe" of all the different asset classes allows us to celebrate the "winners" without being devastated by the "losers."

Now that we have introduced you to the first four important principles of investing—asset allocation, timing and behavior, and rebalancing and diversification—it's now time to dive into understanding and identifying risk. We'll begin with market risk, although, as you'll begin to understand in subsequent chapters, market risk is only the tip of the risk iceberg.

RISK VS. VOLATILITY AND CAPITAL MARKET HISTORY

Is there a difference in the meaning of the words *risk* and *volatility?*

The answer is yes; the difference is subtle, but it's crucial for investors to understand.

- **Risk:** Exposure to the chance of loss; the degree of probability of putting money into an investment that may *permanently* lose all of its value. As an example, the probability of loss when investing in an individual stock (one company) is greater than investing in a fund of many stocks (many companies), where the probability of total, permanent loss of value of all the companies in the fund at once is extremely unlikely.

- **Volatility:** Volatility is how rapidly and dramatically an investment tends to change in price.

If you are worried about the "risk level" of a certain investment, you are worried about the potentially permanent loss of your money. Whereas an investment's volatility should be a concern to investors if the money is needed in the immediate or near-term future.

Just because an investment is more volatile does not necessarily mean it is *risk*ier in the long term. As an investment's time horizon gets longer, the effect of volatility is reduced greatly.

The stock market as a whole is much more volatile than bank CDs or bonds but that does not mean retirees should bypass any investment in the stock market. Instead, it means that investors should know the potential for short-term volatility to affect the value of their investments and plan accordingly.

The best way that we can illustrate both short term volatility and risk is to review how markets have behaved over the last ninety-plus years.

HISTORY AS A GUIDE FOR BETTER DECISIONS

When it comes to investing, the best tool any investor

has at their disposal is the readily available evidence of history, meaning that the future returns from various types of investment asset classes may not exactly repeat themselves, but have historically never deviated wildly from their long-term averages. The data and charts on the following pages represent ninety years of capital market history. Short-term, non-contextualized investment "advice" from the media, well-meaning friends, colleagues and sometimes financial services professionals often loses sight of the patterns in history that are so readily apparent when you take the long-term view into account.

History doesn't repeat itself, but it rhymes. Over the past ninety years, the United States has shifted between different political regimes, contentious political and economic environments, war, terrorism, inflation, booms, busts, and more. Whenever something changes in our society, the media jumps on it as a way to pull in viewers; they spin tales of market woe and oftentimes offer short-term, fear-driven advice. If one simply looks at the long-term view and has a plan in place to handle the short-term volatility, that fear-mongering begins to look downright foolish.

Summary Statistics of Annual Total Returns 1926-2016

Series	Average Return	Volatility
Large company stocks	10.0	19.9
Small company stocks	12.1	31.9
Long-term corporate bonds	6.0	8.4
Long-term government bonds	5.5	9.9
Intermediate-term government bonds	5.1	5.6
US Treasury bills	3.4	3.1
Inflation	2.9	4.1

Source: Ibbotson SBBI 2017 Classic Yearbook © Duff & Phelps

In *Summary Statistics of Annual Total Returns 1926–2016*, we can see the connection between volatility and return. When you look at the annual total returns for the seven major asset classes of the US market over the past ninety years, you can see that those asset classes with a higher average return also exhibit higher volatility.

Let's define what exactly the two columns of data represent. The average return in this chart is the average return over ninety years of data, but as we all probably know, average is anything but average! In any given year, the returns can vary widely. How widely is represented by the volatility number. In the case of large company stocks, it means that in any given year, it can be the average return + or – the volatility number. For example, as you can see in the chart, 10 percent + 19.9 = 29.9 percent or 10 percent – 19.9 percent = -9.9 percent. In more volatile years, it could be 2 times volatility, meaning 10 percent + 39.98 percent = 49.98 percent or 10 percent – 39.98 percent = -29.98 percent. We have even seen 3 times volatility, most recently during the Great Recession in 2008. If you look further down the chart, you can see that intermediate-term government bonds have a much smaller average return of 5.1 percent, but the volatility of this asset class is accordingly much lower as well, at 5.6 percent.

Now, let's also take a look at inflation, which runs on average 2.9 percent during this timeframe, but has a volatility factor of 4.1 percent. To illustrate the volatility of inflation, we assume most reading this book can remember the late 1970s and early 1980s when inflation ran much higher than the average. Remember the high mortgage rates and long gas lines? The important information to glean from this chart is as follows: if you need to grow an income in order to keep pace with inflation over a multi-decade retirement, you will need to accept some level of volatility in your portfolio.

INFLATION AND OMELETS

Consider one of the most important factors that must be recognized when devising a retirement income and investment strategy: protecting your purchasing power for upwards of three decades.

To understand the importance of protecting your purchasing power throughout your retirement, a helpful analogy is that of an omelet; imagine the cost of a single omelet.

After the Great Depression, you could go to your favorite diner, put forty-five cents down on the counter, and they'd cook you an omelet. Over the course of the twentieth century, that price rose. Now, almost ninety years later, your forty-five cents won't even buy you an additional filling, and you'll need somewhere around sixteen dollars to purchase the entire omelet. From forty-five cents to sixteen dollars—that's a huge increase. It represents the cost of the omelet doubling about *five times* over the course of ninety years.

The omelet gets more expensive across those decades due to inflation. Most people know what inflation is: it's the basic economic concept that things get more expensive as time goes on. However, inflation isn't something one can witness as readily and abruptly as, say, a sudden plunge in the price of stocks. Inflation, as we mentioned previously, is more like carbon monoxide—odorless and undetectable, but if ignored, disastrous to your future.

Consider this graph, which represents the historical measures of inflation throughout the twentieth century and beginning of the twenty-first century.

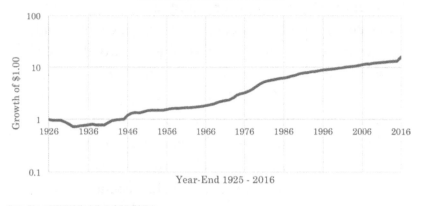

Inflation: Cumulative Index

Growth of $1.00

Year-End 1925 - 2016

Source: Ibbotson SBBI 2017 Classic Yearbook © Duff & Phelps

This graph illustrates the difference, due to inflation, of the price of your omelet over a long period of time. You can see the rise from $1 to $16 over the course of ninety years; you can see the difference, even between the cost of the omelet in 1986 and the cost of the omelet in 2016, over a thirty-year span that corresponds to a typical retirement timeline.

The protection of your purchasing power—your ability to maintain your lifestyle on Day 1 of your retirement just as well as twenty to thirty years in the future should be your top priority. In reality, many retirees through lack of planning as well as lack of education of the various risks retirees face, do not adequately plan for growing income in such a way that it can double and almost triple over several decades.

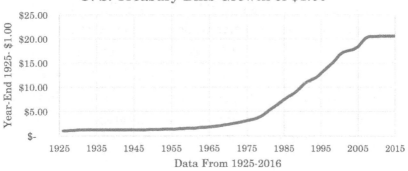

U. S. Treasury Bills Growth of $1.00

Data From 1925-2016

CASH: IS IT REALLY A SAFE HAVEN?

Now, let's take a look at what most retires would refer to as the "safest" investment, money in the bank.

Retirees worry about risk. They think, *it's taken me a lifetime to accumulate this money, and I can't lose it; I have to live on it for the rest of my life.* The typical retiree wants a safe thirty-year place to put their money. What we came to realize is that this retiree is confusing their retirement *date* with their retirement *timeframe.* They may retire when they're sixty-two, which is their retirement date; however, their retirement timeframe is potentially twenty-five or thirty years into the future.

Cash seems safe; if it's in the bank, its value should rise steadily over the decades. By keeping their money in cash, retirees avoid the risk they detect in investments like bonds or stocks. Retirees, who are programmed to believe they have a limited runway to withstand market volatility, love to believe that they can put all their money somewhere they perceive to be safe. In the graph *U.S. Treasury Bills Growth of $1.00*, we see $1 invested in a savings account, a bank CD, etc. in 1926. Over the course of ninety years, this $1 grew to $20! On the surface, this seems appealing; I can still eat my omelet at $16 and have little to no risk. *Sign me up!*

However, this doesn't tell the whole story.

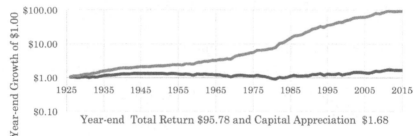

Intermediate-Term Government Bonds: Return Indices, Returns and Yields

Year-end Total Return $95.78 and Capital Appreciation $1.68

This graph shows the truth of what a long-term investment in intermediate-term government bonds looks like. But first, it's important to understand what exactly a bond is. Most simply put, bonds represent debt obligations, and are therefore a form of borrowing. If a company issues a bond, the money they receive in return is a loan, and must be repaid over time. Just like the mortgage on a home or a credit card payment, the repayment of the loan also entails periodic interest to be paid to the lenders. Investors, as the buyers of bonds, then, are essentially lenders. For example, if you have ever bought a government savings bond, you became a lender to the federal government. Put differently, bonds are IOUs—whereas stocks are a form of company ownership.

The top line of the chart represents the growth of one dollar invested in intermediate-term government bonds over ninety years. As you can see, that dollar grows to about $100.00. A retiree may now think that bonds are an excellent investment—certainly, far better than cash, which only grew to $20.00 over the same ninety years. It's important to note, however, that this top line in the graph assumes that all of the interest payments received from the bonds were reinvested.

The bottom line of this graph shows a dollar invested in the same bonds in 1926, but with the interest income not reinvested, but removed to pay for living expenses. Without that interest income reinvested into the bonds, the investment doesn't grow to $100; in fact, it barely grows at all! By 2016, your 1926 dollar is worth only $1.68, not the $16 it needs to reach to buy your omelet. Now, let's go back and think about the cash in the bank and your $1 invested in 1926. If you had to live off of the interest of that investment—meaning the bank interest was removed instead of left to compound over the years—you actually would have lost money! How will you buy that omelet now?

Relative to *short-term* market risk, cash and bonds are safe and have a place in your portfolio. But relative to maintaining your *purchasing power*, having all of your money in cash and bonds isn't safe at all. In fact, it's downright risky. For generations, retirees have been programmed to believe that the best course to follow is to de-risk their portfolios in retirement. However, as we have illustrated throughout this book, the baby boomer generation is redefining investing in retirement in light of their new reality: retirements lasting upwards of thirty years and healthcare expenses increasing at a rate more than double inflation.

What is the only investment that, over a lengthy time horizon, has consistently beaten inflation and allowed portfolios to keep pace with the rate of health-care expenses?

STOCKS: NOT AS RISKY AS YOU THINK

Now let's take a look at an investment often feared to be too risky for retirees to own in any significant percentage.

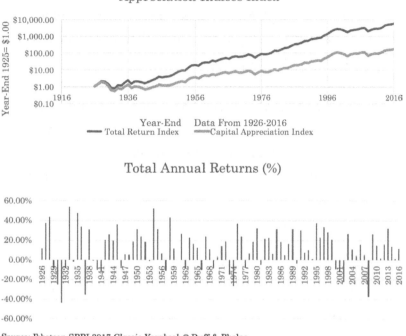

Large Company Stocks: Total Return and Capital Appreciation Indices Index

Year-End 1925= $1.00

Year-End Data From 1926-2016
— Total Return Index ▬▬Capital Appreciation Index

Total Annual Returns (%)

Source: Ibbotson SBBI 2017 *Classic Yearbook* © Duff & Phelps

This graph shows what happens if a person invests their dollar into large company stocks over the same ninety-year period. The growth is significant, especially compared to the growth of both the cash account and bonds examined previously; when capital gains and dividends are continuously reinvested, the dollar in 1926 grows to nearly $10,000 in 2016. Most importantly, the bottom line of this graph shows that even if this person does *not* continuously reinvest the capital gains and dividends, and instead uses that income for living expenses, the dollar in 1926 still grows to $100 in 2016. Remember, stocks are a form of ownership; they represent participation in a company's growth or decline. Ownership allows you to participate in the appreciation of a company, where bonds, as a debt obligation, do not.

If a retiree can accept the short-term volatility that accompanies stock (as illustrated by the chart, "Annual Returns"), follows the investment fundamentals outlined earlier and has a plan in place to manage the other risks unique to a retiree that we discuss in the next chapter, purchasing power can be protected.

While the psychology of a typical retiree includes the instinct to safeguard their nest egg in a low-risk investment like a cash account or bonds, what we've shown is that the seemingly *riskiest* place to put their money—the stock market—is indeed the most likely by far to protect their ability to buy their omelet throughout their retirement. It's important to understand that the psychology of risk avoidance will likely lead you to make a decision with your money that could seriously harm your ability to maintain your lifestyle.

Understand that you will need to accept certain levels of volatility in your portfolio in order to garner the returns that will both keep pace with inflation while also allowing your income to grow. Understanding the level of volatility that you need to tolerate in order to achieve your goals, and what you can emotionally accept without reverting to emotionally triggered behavior, will be an important part of building your income and investment strategy.

ASSET ALLOCATION REVISITED: TIME TO MAKE AN INFORMED DECISION

Deciding what your allocation should be across stocks, bonds, and cash, the first step is to balance these two key metrics: historical rate of return—versus historical volatility. When viewed this way, risk tolerance becomes a rational, rather than emotional, decision. And, when looking at the predictable relationship between rate of return and volatility through the long-term lens of history, most investors find that they are emotionally able to tolerate a higher level of risk than they had previously believed.

Consider the historical returns on various stock/bond portfolio allocations:

12-Month Modeled & Historical Returns on Various Stock/Bond Allocations

	Long-term Corporate Bonds	Large Company Stock	Historical Return 1926-2016	Historical Volatility (One Std Deviation Range)	Historical Range 1926-2016
1	100	0	6%	-2.4% to 14.4%	-8.1% to 42.6%
2	60	40	7.6%	-5.4% to 20.6%	-22.2% to 47.1%
3	50	50	8%	-6.2% to 22.2%	-25.7% to 48.3%
4	40	60	8.4%	-6.9% to 23.7%	-29.2% to 49.4%
5	30	70	8.8%	-7.7% to 25.3%	-32.8% to 50.6%
6	20	80	9.2%	-8.4% to 26.8%	-36.3% to 51.7%
7	0	100	10%	-9.9% to 29.9%	-43.3% to 54%

Source: Ibbotson SBBI 2017 Classic Yearbook © Duff & Phelps

As you can see from line 1 of the chart, a portfolio with 100 percent allocated to bonds and 0 percent allocated to stocks averaged the lowest returns from 1926 to 2016 (6 percent); however, this allocation also had the advantage of the lowest volatility. As you move down the chart, let's say to line 5, which shows a 30 percent bond, 70 percent stock allocation, you can see higher returns and as you expect, the corresponding higher volatility. When trying to make an asset allocation decision—such as, "should I have 60 percent in stock or 70 percent in stock"—we like clients to focus on the column furthest to the right, entitled "Historical Range." This column represents your worst-case scenario over the past ninety years. What experience tells us is that if you can understand and emotionally accept that your portfolio may and probably will go down 36 percent at some point in the future, then you can better make the decision to take on this risk level. For example, here are real numbers for a better perspective: your $1,000,000 portfolio just lost $360,000 in value, meaning its value has declined to $640,000. Remember, if you do nothing and you choose to give your portfolio the time it needs to recover, this decline in value is a "paper loss" only. If history is our guide, the losses are temporary and the gains over the long term are permanent. Unless you make the irrevocable decision to panic and sell, your portfolio, given time, will recover, assuming you are following the investment fundamentals we have outlined for you. None of the allocations on this chart is necessarily the "right" one. It's important for each individual investor to decide how much market risk they are willing and able to tolerate, and plan their allocation accordingly.

Investing requires risk. There is no way to avoid it. However, market risk as dealt with in this chapter hardly tells the whole story. In order to make this asset allocation decision with a 360-degree view, it is necessary to understand *all* the risks a retiree faces.

In the next chapter, we will illustrate how market risk is both manageable and from our perspective not the most important, risk a retired investor needs to be concerned with.

CHAPTER FIVE

<hr>

MARKETS AND INVESTMENTS: HOW TO MANAGE RISK

What do we mean when we talk about risk?

Most people's minds immediately jump to the stock market, and the inherent unpredictability and volatility of investing. They'd be correct to assume that market risk is something for which they need to plan carefully in their retirement. However, market risk should not be any retired investor's sole focus.

One of our clients, Jay, and his wife, Susan, began their retirement planning in, all things considered, pretty good shape. During their working years, they had accumulated two million dollars and felt reasonably confident that this was going to be enough money.

When we began working with them, one of the first things we noticed was that their portfolio was still structured much in the same way that it was in their accumulation years, which is fairly common. However, what got them there may not have served them well in their distribution years. As they neared their retirement transition, they were correct to assume they should revisit their asset allocation decision to determine their investment strategy going forward; but they also needed to make some additional changes. What they failed to think about was how they should structure their portfolio in their distribution years so that it had the ability to produce a growing stream of income that would keep pace with the normal cost-of-living increases, and even further help handle healthcare costs in the future.

RISK GOES BEYOND THE MARKET

One thing that is certain is that risk will always be a factor. However, it doesn't have to derail your retirement. Just like any other aspect of this process, the course that will provide you with the most confidence and the least stress is to develop a plan.

As a person accumulates wealth throughout their working years, they weather certain investment risks—for the most part, these risks have to do with the stock market and unforeseen volatility and the behavior that it drives. More significantly, when a typical working adult in their thirties or forties sets up and maintains their retirement accounts, they're not often well-educated as to what exactly they're planning *for*.

In contrast to the accumulation phase's short-term risk of market volatility, the risks during a retiree's distribution phase are different, and wholly unique to retirement.

Risks of Retirement

Withdrawals
- **What rate is sustainable?**
- **Sequencing by tax bracket**
- **Managing RMDs**

Longevity
- **Retirement horizons: couple aged 65 has 25% chance of survivor living to age 96**

Spending
- Replacement ratio
- Essential vs lifestyle expenses
- Medical expenses

Retirement income

Taxes
- **Asset allocation**
- **Accelerating income**
- **Partial Roth conversions**

Market volatility
- **Uncertain returns and income**
- **Impact of point in time**
- **Asset allocation and location**

Inflation
- **Erodes the value of savings and reduces returns**

Savings
- Under-funded defined contribution accounts
- Most Americans have an enormous savings gap

To most retirees that we've worked with, the real risks of the distribution phase are not well-known. However, with an understanding of what these unique risks entail, careful effort put into planning, and a process for handling these risks, they can be marginalized, and even mitigated.

DISTRIBUTION PHASE: SOME RISKS ARE FAMILIAR, SOME ARE NOT

When planning for the future, the uncertainty presented to the retiree is both inevitable and unknown; all that *is* known is that uncertainty is a definite component of any person's retirement years. Furthermore, so many of the factors that affect a person in their retirement—their health, family, domestic and global politics and economics, world events—are inherently unpredictable, and represent a wide landscape of possibilities for disruption in future years.

That said, there are five main risks that every retiree should factor into their planning when looking ahead to retirement. There are market and withdrawal risks, which are short-term in general, and inflation and longevity risks, which are longer-term. Tax risk tends to straddle both the shorter- and longer-term risk timeframe.

In the coming sections, we will outline ways to manage these risks. But first, we'll explore each of these risks in depth. It's crucial to remember that, when creating a retirement income plan, the stakes are high. There will be very little space to course-correct in the future, so getting the plan right from the outset should be the focus of every person entering retirement.

The good news is that, through this careful planning, risk transforms from something unpredictable—even scary—into something you can effectively plan for and thereby manage.

MARKET RISK

On some level, everyone believes they understand market risk. *You invest in a stock, and there's always the risk that stock could go down in value or, worse, become worthless.*

What we often see people mistaking about market risk is its relative weight when compared to the other four risks of the distribution phase. People tend to fear market risk more immediately and place its mitigation as their top priority above the other risks of the distribution phase.

Recall how, in the previous chapter, we talked about how many retirees weight their focus solely on market risk. They confuse their retirement *date* with their retirement, income, and investment *timeline*.

Also, recall the frequent confusion of *volatility* and *loss*. Loss is simple: if you are unable to recover your money—"I own a stock and it went to zero"—you lost. Whereas if your portfolio declines—even precipitously—that's just a decline. Assuming that you have a well-thought-out income and investment strategy and are applying the fundamentals we outlined in the previous chapter, given time, your portfolio will recover. Why do we say that? Simply because there has never been a time in our history when that hasn't happened!

WITHDRAWAL RISK AND THE ODDS OF GETTING BACK TO EVEN

Withdrawal risk is one that nearly every client we work with hasn't considered. But it's very real, and can have adverse consequences to any retiree if not managed, especially those who have several decades of income to plan for.

Withdrawal risk has to do solely with the need to take money out of your investment portfolio when the markets are down. Recall the distinction between volatility and loss; if you've not accounted for withdrawal risk, and you have to take out money when the market is down, you'll be forced to sell pieces of your portfolio to do so—and you'll need to sell them at a loss. That can be very damaging to the overall longevity of your portfolio.

This table shows what happens when an investor with

a portfolio worth $500,000 withdraws 5 percent, or $25,000, per year and they haven't accounted for withdrawal risk.

Market Volatility and a Portfolio Providing Income in Retirement

$500,000 initial balance, first year (and subsequent years) end of year withdrawal of $25,000.

Portfolio Loss	Required Annual Return to Get to Even Within 3 Years	Required Annual Return to Get to Even Within 5 Years
-5%	10.9%	8.0%
-10%	14%	9.7%
-20%	22%	13.5%
-25%	26.5%	15.5%
-35%	37%	20.6%

Source: Portfolio of retirement investor in withdrawal mode. Assumes a $500,000 initial balance, first year end of year withdrawal of 5%, $25,000 of initial balance. $25,000 is also withdrawn subsequent years.

This table illustrates a retired investor with a $500,000 portfolio invested in 60 percent stock and 40 percent bonds. Each year, he takes out $25,000 in order to supplement his other sources of income. What this investor hasn't thought about, or hasn't developed a plan for, is withdrawing that income in years when the markets are down. If you look at the chart, when his portfolio has declined 20 percent (and with a 60 percent stock portfolio, this investor will see this sort of decline during his twenty- to thirty-year retirement) and he had to withdraw $25,000 to create income, in order to get his portfolio back to even, he would need a return of 22 percent over the next three years, and 13.5 percent over the next five years.

Refer back to the chart at the end of chapter 4 entitled *12 Month Modeled and Historical Returns on Various Stock/Bond Allocations*. If you were to look at what a 60 percent stock, 40 percent bond portfolio has returned on average over the last ninety years, you can see it is 8.4 percent. Now, to think that a portfolio that has historically averaged 8.4 percent will somehow return 22 percent over the next three years, or 13.5 percent over the next five years, would be failing to pay attention to the facts; history tells us this would be highly improbable. Therefore, without having a strategy in place to manage this withdrawal risk, you may end up going into principal in years when markets are down, and it will be very hard to recover after you have had to sell and lock in those losses.

In our experience, most retirees would be well advised to be aware of and manage the risk of the markets, but also objectively recognize that the only way they are going to create a growing stream of income is to have exposure, in a thoughtful and diversified way, to stocks.

Ultimately, by developing a plan to handle both volatility and the need to create an income that grows, you will ensure that you have managed the two short-term risks a retiree faces: market risk and withdrawal risk. Fortunately, there's a simple step-by-step way to manage these risks that we'll lay out in the next chapter, and if you follow those steps, volatility and withdrawal risk can be mitigated.

Now let's begin to look at the longer-term risks, starting with inflation.

INFLATION RISK: PROTECT YOUR PURCHASING POWER

Because inflation isn't as sharply apparent as sudden market shifts, most people tend to dismiss inflation risk when compared with market risk. During an investor's working years, they tend to miss the creep upward of their daily expenses, because while items get more expensive to purchase year after year, most people are also likely making more money year after year; the pain, therefore, isn't as apparent as the volatility they experience in their 401(k) when it declines.

Talk to anyone who has been retired for five years or more, however, and they'll tell you a different story about inflation. They have a different perspective now that they're living on somewhat of a fixed income, and the savings they've accumulated for this stage of their life is all they have. If they've done their planning right, and they've carefully considered the steady rise in living expenses, their retirement plan should be solid. However, those who don't think about inflation, and who don't factor it in as one of the major risks of retirement, usually will find themselves dipping into principal year over year just to keep pace with their expenses.

It isn't as simple as coming up with an income number and sticking to it for the length of your retirement, meaning that if you need $25,000 per year today, you cannot simply plan for an income of $25,000 for the next twenty years. Recall that you didn't notice inflation as much during your working years, because your income was rising right alongside it. The same must be true in your retirement; your income has to increase with cost-of-living increases, at a minimum. Whatever your income is on day one of your retirement, it'll need to be *double* and maybe even triple that over the course of three-plus decades.

Here's an example: let's say that tomorrow is the first day of your retirement. You've defined your goals, done your budgeting, and you've come up with a figure of needing to generate $50,000 a year from your investments to maintain your lifestyle. You'll set up regular disbursements from your investment accounts equal to $4,166 per month, and seemingly, you'll be set for retirement. However, things aren't that simple.

Due to inflation, ten years from now, that $50,000 will need to grow to $67,851 in order to buy the same goods and services. Ten years later, that $67,851 will need to grow to $92,075.34. Ten years after that, it will need to grow to nearly $125,000!

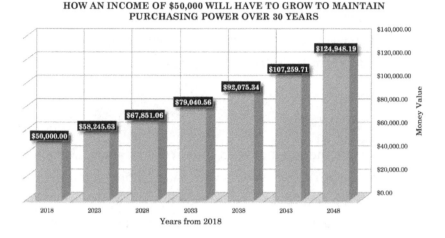

HOW AN INCOME OF $50,000 WILL HAVE TO GROW TO MAINTAIN PURCHASING POWER OVER 30 YEARS

As you can see in this chart, a retiree who begins their distribution phase with a $50,000 income need from savings will need to grow that amount to nearly $125,000 over the thirty years of their retirement. If they fail to plan for this, their purchasing power by the end of their retirement may have been cut in half.

Any retiree's number-one objective should simply be making sure they have a growing stream of income in retirement so that they can maintain their standard of living in year ten, year twenty, year thirty, and beyond. It's important to shift your mindset *away* from protecting your principal, and *toward* protecting your purchasing power. If you begin with a portfolio of $500,000, and all you focus on is protecting that sum, you'll be left behind by the rising tide of inflation. Whereas if you focused on protecting your purchasing power—protecting your ability to buy an omelet at any time in the future—it forces you to put your efforts into growing your nest egg in order to build a growing stream of income for life.

LONGEVITY RISK

There's a fine line between inflation risk and longevity risk. Both concepts deal with the risk presented by increasing costs over time. Longevity risk, however, is exactly what it sounds like, living longer than expected; and along with an extended advanced age comes the increased probability of ever-rising healthcare expenses.

There is no one easy solution to deal with these costs. One can never accurately forecast what the future will bring, but there are some reasonably practical ways of estimating these expenses. Vanguard has produced a whitepaper entitled "Planning for Healthcare costs in Retirement." This white paper estimates that a typical sixty-five-year-old will spend, on average, $5,200 per year on healthcare costs. This is in addition to Medicare premiums, supplemental insurance premiums, and Medicare surcharges where they apply. Some retirees will maintain excellent health until the end of life, while some will see a steady decline in health and quality of life and will spend more and more on healthcare. Others may experience a catastrophic health event and need some sort of nursing home care, which is ultimately the most expensive and thereby damaging to any well-thought-out financial plan. Further complicating this, in our experience, is the fact that there is no one right answer for everyone.

Sometimes it's hard for clients to envision experiencing a catastrophic health event; the very subject makes some people very uncomfortable. Others may be open to beginning the discussion because they have lived through this experience with their own parents and have seen firsthand what was at stake when there was no preparation or plan developed. Whichever camp a retiree falls into, when they do want to address the issue, we generally recommend one of three choices: the purchase of long-term care insurance; the self-funding of future healthcare expenses, which may involve the use of irrevocable trusts or may not; or a combination of the two.

What approach will work best is always situational, so again, there is no one right answer for everyone. Our firm recommendation is to factor this risk into your planning so that you can get a picture of the dollar implications should a healthcare event become your reality. The current data shows that as a retiree gets older, there is a high likelihood of healthcare costs becoming a larger and larger percentage of their annual expenses. These healthcare costs rise at a dramatically faster rate than the average rate of inflation; currently, healthcare costs are rising by an average of 8 percent to 11 percent annually.[3]

In fact, these studies show that in the last decade of people's lives, the amount they need to spend on healthcare is immensely higher than at any other time in their lives. If you don't factor in this rise in healthcare costs, it could have negative implications for yourself, your spouse, extended family, and overall legacy goals.

TAX RISK

When creating income in retirement, the sequencing of your withdrawals, (which means where you to take the money from and when) along with the decisions you make regarding how and when to claim social security along with some other pertinent factors, can have a large impact on the amount of taxes you will be required to pay both today and in the future.

Prior to retirement—and prior to social security benefits and required minimum distributions of retirement accounts—for the typical W2 worker, there's not a lot of tax planning to be done. When you retire, however, and

---

3   Vanguard Research, "Global Active Bond Fund Returns: A Factor
     Decomposition." https://advisors.vanguard.com/iwe/pdf/ISGGAB.
     pdf?cbdForceDomain=true&EXCMPGN=EX:PC:FAS:Sustaining

when income sources like social security come into the picture, tax planning becomes much more pertinent, and can be extremely impactful—either positively or negatively—on the amount of taxes you pay each year and over your lifetime. This impact has to do with the interplay between how all your income sources are taxed. It's not uncommon, therefore, for people to be paying significantly more tax than they had anticipated. In many cases, because of lack of planning, they're paying it unnecessarily.

Before you retire, assuming you are a W2 employee, you are working within a two-bracket system: income and capital gains. Once you retire and start collecting social security, you introduce provisional income, acting as a third bracket, and another set of calculations come into the picture. Remember the old adage: *two's company, three's a crowd*? Well, income, capital gains, and provisional income don't always play nice together, often creating significantly higher rates of tax. Further complicating this is the fact that at the age of seventy and a half, required minimum distributions (RMDs) begin. The addition of RMDs creates the very real potential to subject the average retiree to sometimes significantly higher tax brackets, additional Medicare surcharges, net investment income taxes, and the dreaded alternative minimum tax.

For years, people have listened to the conventional

wisdom of how to claim social security and how to spend down your assets, meaning they were told to take social security early and spend taxable money first, then tax-deferred money, and tax-free money (like a Roth IRA) last. Experience now tells us that this conventional wisdom may result in significantly higher tax bills. It is not uncommon for us to see where people can save hundreds of thousands of tax dollars over their retirement by making well-informed, well-planned decisions. Due to the fact that everyone's tax situation is so unique to them and the tax code is forever changing, there is no one-size-fits-all solution or approach. In fact, even a highly customized strategy will need to be re-evaluated year to year.

Generally speaking, when converting savings to income, the simplest way of determining where to take dollars from in any given year will be by getting clear around the tax bracket you are in today versus what bracket you think you may be in tomorrow. It is our belief that federal tax rates will be higher in the future when the Tax Cut and Jobs Act of 2017 sunsets in 2025; even if they don't raise taxes at that time, many retirees will find themselves pushed into a higher tax bracket tomorrow due to the interplay of what in essence is a three-bracket system and Required Minimum Distributions. Due to all of this, we believe that a perfect storm exists for the many recently retired and about to be retired.

At this phase in your life, you would be advised to explore the tax planning opportunities that may exist, the feasibility of accelerating income to fill up lower tax brackets, partial Roth IRA conversions, various product selection, asset location, and the various ways of sequencing withdrawals.

ONE MORE RISK: SPENDING TOO MUCH

There is one last risk that we should address before we begin to speak about risk management, and that is overspending.

The big question we are often asked is, "How much can we spend?" All the care you take in developing a retirement income and investment plan will be of no use if you spend more from your portfolio than what is *sustainable* in the long term. This means that if you spend too much year over year, you risk the chance of your portfolio not lasting the thirty or more years you may need it to. Without a plan in place that incorporates a sustainable spending rate, it can become a footrace as to what happens first: your money runs out, or your life runs out. Understanding what is in play here is important, and oftentimes, we find that people do not know how to determine what is a safe withdrawal rate from a retirement portfolio.

There is a simple rule of thumb to calculate how much

annual income can be withdrawn from investments: the 4.15 percent rule. This rule states that a sustainable, growing income can be maintained by spending 4.15 percent of your savings per year.

For example, if you have a total portfolio value of $1,000,000, you can withdraw $41,500 each year to supplement your other forms of income. You'll have the ability to grow that income over the years to keep pace with inflation, and if the rules we outline here are followed, you should not have to worry about running out of money.[4]

This rule assumes a few things: first, that you are invested somewhere between 37 percent and 67 percent in stocks, depending on your risk tolerance; second, that you strategically rebalance your portfolio at least annually; third, that your portfolio is properly diversified; and fourth, that you have set up a process to help manage the various risks unique to a retiree (which we will discuss next).

If these assumptions are true, then spending becomes a simple multiplication problem: in our example of a $1,000,000 portfolio, $1,000,000 × 4.15 percent = $41,500, meaning you have $41,500 as an annual sustainable withdrawal amount you can generate from your investments. You can also use this rule to calculate how

---

4   William P. Bengen, CFP, *Conserving Client Portfolios During Retirement*

big of a nest egg you need. If you know that you will need an income of $41,500 from your savings, you can do a division problem to figure out how much you should accumulate: $41,500 / 4.15 percent = $1,000,000.

The 4.15 percent rule is not without its critics. Our stance is that, away from academia and in the real world, the 4.15 percent rule is a great starting point for calculating sustainable withdrawals. We've seen clients achieve great success using it as a simple calculation to solidify their retirement income plans.

PRACTICAL RISK MANAGEMENT

Now that you understand the core unique risks of the distribution phase, it's important to figure out how to tackle them.

Timing and prioritization are crucial. For example, these five core risks arise at different times during retirement; as such, they should be dealt with in accordance with that timing. There are two primary categories these risks fall into: *short-term risks* and *long-term risks*.

Short-term risks:

- Market risk
- Withdrawal risk

Long-term risks:

- Inflation risk
- Longevity risk

You may be wondering where tax risk fits in; taxes, interestingly, are both a short-term and long-term risk.

Although it requires some effort and careful planning to account for these risks in your retirement, once they have been properly planned for, these risks largely become psychological and emotional, rather than economic or financial.

The most important thing to remember about risk is that it can be managed and accounted for with prudent planning. Risk implies an unknown; it is inevitable that the retiree will face moments of uncertainty in the decades to come. By creating a retirement plan that not only leaves space for, but accounts for, that uncertainty, the retiree can feel confident that their retirement years will weather whatever comes their way.

BUCKETS OF MONEY

We've mentioned how the unique risks of the distribution phase—market, withdrawal, inflation, longevity, and tax—can be mitigated with a well-structured and properly sequenced distribution plan. But what does this actually look like in practice?

George and Mary, a couple in their late fifties, were beginning to plan for retirement. George had recently been downsized at work very abruptly, but Mary was still working. Their concerns around retirement were very similar to what we usually hear: Do we have enough? How do we go about creating an income? What happens if the markets go down? Can we afford to take on market risk? George's situation had changed so quickly they hadn't really thought through what their income needs were going to be in retirement. One of the first things we worked with them on was their retirement budget. How much income were they going to need coming in the door in order to maintain their lifestyle? This amount was going to drive a whole host of other decisions: when and how to claim social security, how much longer Mary was going to work, and how were they going to structure their investment portfolio?

After reviewing their budget, they established that they needed $40,000 of additional income from their invest-ments. The first thing we advised them to do was to move between two to three years of this needed income into a very conservative, very liquid account. We call this bucket 1, or the income bucket. We explained to them that this would eliminate the short-term risks of market and withdrawal risk as we discussed earlier in this chapter. As fate would have it, we had this conversation in late 2007. This one decision turned out to be a game changer. As we illustrated in the last chapter, had this income bucket not been established, they would have been forced to sell some of their investments to create needed income in a market that was rapidly declining. That would have left George and Mary with both significantly fewer assets and markedly less retirement income.

In the next section, we will further explain how structuring your savings into different "buckets" will be an effective way to manage risk, not only market and withdrawal risk, but for inflation and longevity risk as well!

TIME-SEGMENTED BUCKETS OF MONEY

First, stop and review: what is most retiree's biggest goal? To maintain their lifestyle in retirement. In order to do this, they will need to receive a steady, stable, predictable. and growing income. A portion of that income, for most people, will need to be generated from savings. In order to keep that income predictable and consistent, we must have a plan in place to manage the five risks we've outlined earlier. The best way we have found to manage these unique risks, and the method we have implemented in our client's accounts for decades, is a process we call "Buckets of Money."

Income

Growth and
income

Long-term
liquidity

Cash and short-term
bonds

Blended, moderate/growth-
oriented portfolios

Growth portfolios

Your money throughout your retirement will be divided into three buckets, each representing a period of time: short term, medium term, and long term. Each bucket is responsible for managing a specific risk(s).

BUCKET 1: INCOME—MANAGING MARKET AND WITHDRAWAL RISK

In bucket number one, we keep anywhere from one to upwards of three years of planned cash flow in investments that are highly conservative and highly liquid. For example, with George and Mary, they need $40,000 per year from their investments. We would keep anywhere from $40,000 to upwards of $120,000 in this bucket. Why? This is money that we know we need to take out to pay the electric and buy food and maintain their lifestyle. We need this income regardless of what the markets are doing; therefore, it should not be subject to the volatility of the markets. We can withdraw our $40,000 each year and not have to worry about market risk or withdrawal risk. Why do we recommend having three years' worth of income in this bucket? Because we have not experienced a market downturn where it has not begun to recover within three years.

BUCKET 2: GROWTH AND INCOME—MANAGING INFLATION RISK AND TOMORROW'S INCOME NEEDS

Bucket 2 is where the bulk of your money will go. It will be fully invested in accordance with your asset allocation decision, i.e., 60 percent stocks, 40 percent bonds or 70 percent stocks, 30 percent bonds, etc.). This bucket has two very important roles: (1) It needs to grow over the long-term to help manage inflation risk (remember, we have to have a plan in place to double and possibly nearly triple our income over a thirty-year retirement) and (2) At appropriate times, it has to re-fill bucket 1, the income bucket, so that there is always adequate money available to generate income that is needed. Refilling bucket 1, the income bucket, is not an exact science, and is perhaps the most critical component of the bucket process. It is a balance between refilling buckets when markets are on the upswing and not letting your bucket 1 get too depleted. As an example, at the end of 2017, a year of spectacular returns in stock, we refilled all of our distribution clients' bucket 1. We weren't trying to time the market; we had no idea if it was at a high or if markets could still go higher. What we knew was that there was growth in bucket 2 and we utilized some of it to refill bucket 1.

BUCKET 3: LONG-TERM LIQUIDITY—MANAGING LONGEVITY RISK AND HANDLING THE UNEXPECTED

This bucket is all about longevity risk, which means healthcare costs and unplanned expenses that could pop up during a thirty-plus year retirement. As a general rule, we calculate what we would need to invest in today's dollars in order to have it grow to the client's original principal amount over thirty years. Typically, most retirees have a desire to never touch their principal. In reality, rarely is that an option over a multi-decade timeframe. So, what we advise is if you were to come to us with $1,000,000, we would put the amount in bucket 3 today that would provide you with the best chance of growing that initial investment back to $1,000,000 in thirty years. Now, depending on how this money is invested, the amounts can vary, but many clients are surprised by how small the amount is. Remember, we have no plan to touch this account for many years to come! We view this bucket as the "Life Happens" bucket. We don't know what, if any, unforeseen healthcare crises there may be in the future. We don't know with any degree of certainty how long someone will live. We don't know what unexpected events may happen. Regardless of how well-thought-out and executed your plan might be, the only certainty is uncertainty!

STRESS-FREE DISTRIBUTION

Although most find the concept of these buckets simple to understand, *simple* doesn't equate to *easy*. The buckets system isn't magic—it doesn't completely eliminate market, withdrawal, inflation, and longevity risk, but it will help to manage them. And it requires maintenance that some may not feel confident in executing. However, if set up and managed properly, the buckets will reduce much of the stress of uncertainty that many retirees feel heading into their distribution phase.

By segmenting your money into buckets, you'll plan for four of the five major risks of the distribution phase. You'll also create a consistent flow of income that you can rely on, regardless of what markets are doing. Without a bucket strategy, it's difficult to account for risks that arise at different stages of your retirement.

When you know intellectually and emotionally that your income is not subject to the volatility of the market, most clients relax and focus on what's important—growing an income for the rest of their lives. No matter how much you educate yourself on risk, and no matter how much you commit to a long-term view of the markets, any investor, especially when they are retired, still experiences a shock when the markets take a turn. Your goal is to mitigate this shock so that it doesn't make you panic and so your plan doesn't derail.

CHAPTER SIX

PUTTING YOUR PLAN INTO ACTION

Now that you have thought through your retirement goals that require money, and understand the important investment fundamentals and the basics of converting savings to income while managing the various risks a retiree faces, you are now ready to begin pulling the pieces of your retirement income plan together.

THE FIVE-STEP START TO BECOMING RETIREMENT READY

Comprehensive retirement income planning is a highly customized and multi-faceted discipline. If you've read everything prior to this point in the book, you should now have the framework to begin some basic planning; however, a true customized income plan is well beyond the guidelines of this book. This book is geared toward helping pre-retirees and recent retirees think about generating income in retirement. It will hopefully help them begin to assess their readiness to retire, understand what gaps, if any, they may have, and what professional guidance they may require moving forward.

However, we believe that pulling together these five steps will be a highly worthwhile exercise. Incorporating all of the information we've outlined in this book, it will help you develop a sense of where you stand today and what may need your attention in the future in order to reach your goals. Our tool, the Retirement Income Estimator, provides a simple yet effective guideline as you begin.

To access a downloadable version of this tool, go here:

http://www.questcapitalmanagement.com/downloadable-files

Retirement Income Estimator

Estimated annual income: $86,310

1

Cash Flow, Investments, Bank Accounts	
Annual Cash Flow Needs	Estimated Expense
Amount from budget sheets:	$ 63,000.00

2

Annual Budget for Goal Funding	
Goal #1	$ 15,000.00
Goal #2	$ 5,000.00
Goal #3	$ 2,500.00
	$ -
Expenses Total	$ 85,500.00

Retirement Accounts:	
401(k)s, 403(b)s, 457(b)s	$ 565,000.00
IRAs	$ 75,000.00
Roth IRAs	$ 3,500.00

3

Total retirement accounts:	$ 643,500.00
Non-Retirement Accounts:	
Investment accounts	$ 75,000.00
Cash, Mutual Funds, CDs	$ 48,000.00
Other	$
Total non-retirement accounts:	$ 123,500.00
Assets Total	$ 766,500.00

4

Sources of Income	
All Sources of Income in Retirement	Estimated Value
Social security	$ 32,000.00
Social security	$ 16,000.00
Pension	$ 6,500.00
Pension	$
Rental income	$
Part-time work	$
Income Generated from Savings	
4.15% Retirement Accounts*	$ 26,705.25
4.15% Non-Retirement Accounts	$ 5,104.50

5

Retirement Income Total	$ 86,309.75
Annual Income (-) Expenses	$ 809.75

*Gross distribution before tax withholding

THE FIRST STEP

Your first step is to understand your current living expenses. So many soon-to-be and recent retirees tell us, "I just want to be able to maintain my lifestyle," yet they have only a vague idea of how much that lifestyle will cost them. It's crucial to have a solid grasp of how much money you routinely spend right now so that you can have a realistic estimate of what you will need in the future.

Use our budget worksheet to carefully account for the money you spend right now and what is expected to be spent in retirement. One thing must be made very clear: this exercise will be completely meaningless if you aren't thorough. Gather your account statements, pull up your credit card bills, and go line by line. Figure out exactly how much you spend, and at what frequency, on each of the major expense types. Paint a picture of the last twelve months of expenses. This step will be the basis for everything that follows in your plan, so you need to make sure it's an accurate reflection of your spending habits.

Most importantly: *do not underestimate what you spend.* Put aside, for now, your future life goals that require money; put aside any notions of cutting costs in retirement. Stay focused on the present and simply get down on paper your spending. Answer only this question: what does it really cost me to live, exactly as I am living now?

Enter your annual spending amount from your budget sheets in section 1 of the Retirement Income Estimator.

THE SECOND STEP

The next step is to define your goals. We wrote an entire chapter on this because these defined goals can form a large component of your retirement income plan. Think carefully about what you want out of your retirement. Consider any lifelong aspirations you hope to meet, thinking about travel, housing, and gifts to family, etc. Use the Goals Worksheet we provided here in this book and on our website to hone and focus these goals. Remember that your goals should be:

1. **Prioritized:** It's important to understand which goals are the "must haves" and which ones fall into the category of "would be nice" to have. When we say "most important," we are referring to what are those goals that if you didn't achieve them, you wouldn't feel your retirement was as successful as it could have been. It's important to know which parts of your plan are flexible and which parts are not.

2. **Time-specific:** A goal should be time-specific, such as, *I want to retire at age sixty-five,* or *I want to purchase a second home in five years.* Goal planning is all about the timing of your cash flow needs! Take the time to think through when you will need to fund each goal.

3. **Frequency-specific:** A frequency-specific goal outlines how often you'd like to do certain things, like travel. A vague goal of "traveling" isn't specific enough, but "We'd like to take a trip abroad once every two years for the next 10 years," is.

4. **Dollar-specific:** Just like your budgeting work, it's important that you accurately estimate how much the things you want to do in your retirement will cost. "I want to purchase a second home in five years" is less useful to your planning than a more specific, dollar-based goal, like "I would like to purchase a second home in five years, and I would like to purchase it outright, for a cost of $350,000."

5. **Have a back-up plan:** Despite your best planning efforts, nothing is certain. It's important to keep some flexibility in your planning. Perhaps the goal of buying a second home in five years at $350,000 may not be feasible, but buying a home in seven years for $300,000 is.

Once you've defined and determined the cost of your goals, plug those number(s) into section 2 on the Income Estimator.

THE THIRD STEP

Now that you've determined what you need to spend on an annual basis and set your goals, the third step you'll take is to gather all of your banking and investment statements. This includes 401(k), IRA, annuities, stocks, and bonds, CDs, and savings accounts.

Now, divide these statements into two sums:

- The total value of the tax-deferred assets, i.e., 401(k), and your IRA(s)
- The value of all taxable accounts (in both individual and joint accounts held by you and your spouse and trust accounts if applicable). You would also include Roth IRA accounts in this sum.

You'll need to divide your savings into taxable versus tax-deferred money in order to understand the taxes you may need to pay on withdrawals and to plan how best to sequence those withdrawals. Remember, where you withdraw and *when* you withdraw from a particular account can have a significant impact on taxation.

The conventional wisdom is that you should withdraw your taxable money first; for instance, your cash and savings and investments that live in an account other than a retirement account. *Then* you withdraw your tax-deferred money, i.e., your IRAs, 401(k)s, etc., and then you withdraw your tax-free money, like a Roth IRA.

What we find in reality, however, is that the same conventional wisdom often puts the client in a position where they're paying more tax than what is necessary. Our advice is that the way you sequence income from your savings—the order in which you take it out, and where you take it from—requires qualified advice from an advisor who specializes in retirement income planning. Ideally, that person will work hand-in-hand with your CPA, because neither party can create the full picture on their own, and you will need the combined knowledge of their respective disciplines to do so. You, your advisor, and your CPA together will be able to intelligently plan the sequencing of your withdrawals in order to maximize income and minimize taxes, both on a short-term, year-over-year basis, and in the long term.

Take the two sums from all of your statements and enter these in section 3.

THE FOURTH STEP

Now you're ready to take step four: understanding your guaranteed income sources for retirement.

This requires gathering your social security statements and

seeking advice as to how to make the best social security claiming decision. There are countless claiming options, and there is no such thing as a one-size-fits-all plan for social security. Often, the best thing to do for a married couple is for the higher wage earner to delay taking social security. In the case of single individuals who are in good health and have longevity run in their families, they may also be well-advised to review delaying claiming their benefit as well. However, this presents many people with a dilemma—it could lead to over withdrawing from your nest egg in order to bridge the income need, which means you temporarily withdraw more than the sustainable withdrawal rate of 4.15 percent from your investment accounts in order to maximize your social security benefit. It's not unusual for us to advise our clients to do exactly that: temporarily over-withdraw from their savings in order to bridge the gap until they begin taking social security. The advantage to delaying your social security benefit is often well worth this temporary stopgap. Make sure this decision is made in the context of your overall plan. Once made, for the most part, this decision is irreversible.

Another source of guaranteed income you'll want to understand is any pension income that you or your spouse may have. Decisions about your pension payout should also be made in the context of an overall plan. However, within that realm, there is one red flag we want to raise: the insurance/pension trade-off.

Many times, we see clients taking their full pension option. With the choice of this option, upon the death of the spouse covered by the pension, all benefits cease to the surviving spouse. What people do in order to make up the loss of income to the surviving spouse is purchase permanent life insurance, so that when the covered spouse dies, that lost pension income, in theory, is replaced with the life insurance proceeds.

Here's what this looks like in practice: if you have a $50,000 annual pension, and you take the full pension option, that $50,000 in income will cease when the covered spouse dies, and the surviving spouse will need to replace that income. The common strategy proposed is that purchasing a life insurance policy will take care of that deficit.

This *seems* like a good option, but in reality, it can be problematic. From our experience, the insurance proceeds are usually never enough to replace the lost income. For example, you decide to take the full pension option and you pass away. Now, your spouse no longer receives your $50,000 per year pension, and you believe you've covered that loss of income because you purchased a $500,000 life insurance policy. Although we will discuss this further, in order to create sustainable and inflation-adjusted income from this pool of insurance proceeds, you can withdraw around 4.15 percent annually from this amount, assuming it is properly invested, and 4.15 percent of $500,000 is only $20,000 in income—far from the $50,000 they are looking to replace. And, keep in mind that this $30,000 loss of income is on top of the loss of the lower social security benefit.

The second issue we see is that due to the complexity of most permanent life insurance policies, they often are not well understood by the person who is purchasing them. The policy is sold to them by the sales agent, who is often giving advice without all the relevant details of the client's financial picture—as well as a lack of knowledge on how to go about creating a growing stream of income for life. Fully understanding the life insurance policy you're purchasing takes expertise, and it's possible that unless fully understood, you may end up making a pension decision that is irrevocable and purchasing a life insurance policy that will not bridge the income gap.

Our advice is to make an informed choice. Choosing the right pension option is an important decision. Our bias is that we prefer what is usually called "the joint and survivor option"—*not* taking the full single life option on the pension—which means you'll receive less in annual pension benefits. But when the covered spouse dies, the surviving spouse will see no or little (depending on the joint and survivor choice you make) reduction in income from your pension.

At the end of the day, the true value of a pension is how long you can make the pension payments last.

THE FIFTH STEP

The fifth and final step you will take, once you have all of the information from the past four steps, is to decide how everything you've gathered and assessed translates into income; put more simply, this is where you get a clear picture of how you will need to use your savings combined with other sources of guaranteed income to create an income for life.

Many people get to this step and are still a little lost and unsure of where to go next. They ask us, "Okay, I know how much I have, but how much of that can I spend each year and what will my total income look like?"

As we mentioned earlier in the book, there is a simple rule of thumb to calculate income from investments: the 4.15 percent rule. This rule states that a sustainable, growing income can be maintained by spending 4.15 percent of your savings per year. For example, if you have a total portfolio value of $1,000,000, you can withdraw $41,500 each year to supplement your other forms of income, have the ability to grow that income over the years to keep pace with inflation, and if these rules are followed, you should not have to worry about running out of money.

Remember, this assumes a few things: first, that you are invested somewhere between 37 percent and 67 percent in stocks, depending on your risk tolerance; second, that you strategically rebalance your portfolio at least annually; third, that your portfolio is properly diversified; and fourth, that you have set up your buckets to help manage the various risks unique to a retiree.

Now let's pull the pieces together. To complete *your* Retirement Income Estimator, calculate 4.15 percent of your tax-deferred retirement assets and then 4.15 percent of your taxable assets and add the totals of each to section 5. Total your expenses. Total your income. Minus expenses from income. If you are left with a positive number, you are on the right track! If your number is negative, there may be some further work to do. You may have to save more, be flexible with your goals and or your daily spending. Keep in mind, this estimator is a one-dimensional snapshot at best, and it is not intended to replicate comprehensive planning. It is intended to be a simple assessment of your retirement readiness.

ADDRESSING QUESTIONS AND CONCERNS

In our practical, real-world experience, the system we've laid out in this chapter, and explained in detail throughout the rest of this book, is what we have found *works*. If you educate yourself, do your homework, put careful effort

into your budgeting and goal-setting, and formulate your income plan the way we've outlined, you will have the beginnings of a retirement income plan.

Think back to the original questions and concerns presented by soon to be or recent retirees: Do I have enough? Am I ready to retire? Will I run out of money? How do I best structure my portfolio to create income? What happens when the inevitable market downturn happens right before or during my retirement? Pulling these pieces of the retirement income estimator together, along with the investment fundamentals and a process for buckets, will go a long way to answering these questions for you.

Long-time clients of ours, Dennis and Allison, retired in the late 1990s. During their retirement, they've weathered the Tech Wreck, 9/11, and the 2008 financial crisis. Their retirement income plan, which included the investment fundamentals outlined in this book, a withdrawal strategy that incorporated the 4.15 percent rule and buckets of money, and some flexibility throughout the years, has stood the test of what would seem to be a financially rocky time period. They've been happily enjoying their retirement for twenty years now and have traveled extensively abroad and have made it to forty-seven of the fifty-eight national parks in the USA, and their portfolio has more money in it today than when they first retired!

Creating a plan and then being disciplined on following that plan, from our experience, works.

It's up to you to take this knowledge, and the tools we've provided, and put in the effort to begin to set up a retirement as well-planned and as stress-free as possible.

CHAPTER SEVEN

GETTING HELP: DON'T DIY YOUR FUTURE

As we've stressed throughout this book, the distribution phase of your life differs greatly from the accumulation phase in many ways. The most crucial way it differs, though, is that mistakes are far costlier. You have much less room for error because you have less time and a shorter runway in which to correct errors.

For the first time in your life, in the distribution phase, your investments are tied with your income. Indeed, your investments may be what *generates a good portion of* your income, the same way your career generated your income during your working years.

For the first time in your life, you'll need to generate income from your investments, while at the same time managing the multiple risks we've outlined in this book. Additionally, most people—and honestly, most professionals—don't fully grasp the interplay between income, investments, and taxes. Also, remember the mindset of the typical retiree: *I've worked and saved my whole life. I don't want to make any mistakes with this money. It's all I have.*

If we've accomplished one thing up until this point, it's that we hope that we've enabled you to ask better questions—both of yourself and of your advisors.

Our aim with this book is to provide you with the framework and the education to help you become a more empowered participant when you start to plan your retirement finances. However, this isn't a do-it-yourself manual. Because each retiree's situation is unique, there is no one-size-fits-all plan to retirement finances; there is no way to tailor the content in this book to each individual's needs.

For these reasons, we encourage you to regard this book as the first step in retirement income planning, and armed with this knowledge, seek the advice of a qualified financial advisor.

INCOME STRATEGY IS AN ONGOING TASK

Developing a plan is crucially important. Even more crucial, though, is the proper ongoing implementation of that plan. Our experience tells us that even the best of plans never goes exactly as expected. Because of this, you'll need to be able to step back and apply experience, flexibility, and wisdom in order to stay on track when things don't go according to plan.

If we have accomplished just one thing by writing this book, we hope we have illustrated that the *primary* goal that any retiree should be worried about is protecting their purchasing power, but in order to best do that, you need to educate that retiree about the ongoing risks and decisions required in their distribution phase, such as the inevitable market downturns, buckets, rebalancing, diversification, sequencing of withdrawals, and more. They then begin to understand in a more viable manner how to go about ensuring that their income is consistent, predictable, and growing.

From our perspective, we see two types of consumers.

Consumer 1 says, *I've got this. I may need help developing a plan, but once that's done, I'm comfortable implementing the plan and all that entails: diversification, rebalancing, buckets, and sequencing of withdrawals, on my own.*

Consumer 2 says, *I need help developing a plan, and I'll need help with the ongoing implementation of the plan and with all of the various components that are outlined.*

In our experience, the overwhelming majority of consumers cannot successfully create and implement a retirement income plan in a vacuum. Most would like the assistance of a trusted advisor(s) who understands their situation and does a good job of breaking down the complex into education they can relate to. They realize, as they near retirement, that it's all about planning for income needs. It's not uncommon for us to hear that consumers are getting little to no advice on this.

Forty years of combined experience in this industry tells us that even consumers who feel they have a handle on all the issues inherent in retirement many may not see their blind spots, and that the right qualified advice is an investment that can pay huge dividends, no matter which consumer you are.

WHAT QUALIFICATIONS SHOULD YOU LOOK FOR?

You've made the decision to seek professional help with your retirement plan; great decision. Now that you've made that decision, how do you know you're seeking the *right* help?

Let's begin with the professional designations. A qualified financial advisor should hold some combination of the following:

- **CFP:** Certified Financial Planner
- **ChFC:** Chartered Financial Consultant
- **AIF:** Accredited Investment Fiduciary

Now, let's take a look at the fee structure of the financial planner. Your aim should be to find a qualified advisor who is fee-only, not commission-based. A commission-based fee structure is undesirable for you, the consumer, because it sets up a dynamic that is transaction-driven rather than relationship- and advice-driven. The commission-based financial planner gets paid on product sales and transactions, and then later, when you need additional ongoing advice around any of the issues we've discussed in this book, oftentimes you'll find the type and depth of advice you need and expect the may not be available to you.

The key question you should ask as you interview potential financial services professionals is: *how do they get paid?* They should be transparent and articulate around what services they offer and at what cost.

Fee-only financial planners are obligated to act as fiduciaries for their clients; this means that they put their client's interests before their own, and act solely on their client's behalf. Anytime a potential bias or conflict of interest arises, they are obligated to disclose the bias or conflict and be completely upfront with the client about it. This is an important and, in many ways, very personal relationship. As such, any good financial planner will display a level of discernment with the clients they take on. You don't want a financial planner who will work with anyone who walks through their door.

The regulatory environment doesn't necessarily work that well; to be honest, it allows anyone who can pass a series of tests to market themselves as a financial professional. The regulatory environment also doesn't require licensed brokers to be a fiduciary. From a consumer's perspective, this can be detrimental, because next to healthcare, there are no services of greater importance to a consumer than financial planning services.

To sum it up, this is what's important:

- Compensation and how they are compensated
- Degree of specialization
- Personal chemistry and the ability to communicate effectively with each other and alignment of philosophies
- Regulatory record

It's crucial that you carefully consider and compare the qualifications, credentials, experience, character, and regulatory record of any advisor whose services you are considering hiring. When the advisor is well-qualified and experienced, it may prove to be some of the best money you have spent.

When it comes to making your choice, interview your candidates carefully. Ask them about their other clients, and make sure their typical client is one at retirement age. This ensures that the financial planner is focused most closely on the issues that most concern your future. Additionally, any qualified candidate must be able to articulate a clear strategy for retirement income planning that they follow with their clients, and they should follow an established, proven investment philosophy that they can articulate well. Lastly, they should be providers and implementors of *customized* retirement income plans; if experience has taught us anything, it's that each individual or family's situation is unique and cookie-cutter solutions are seldom in the client's best interest.

The bottom line is that engaging the services of a qualified professional may be the most financially sound decision you make for yourself and your family. Vanguard produces a white paper entitled "Quantifying Advisor's Alpha," which researches how advisors could add value through relationship-oriented advice and services such as financial planning, discipline, and guidance, rather than by trying to outperform the market. The research reveals, year after year, that these types of services offered by qualified professionals can add, all totaled, about 3 percent in returns annually for clients; however, the actual amount of value added may vary significantly, depending on clients' circumstances.

Our hope is that you will allow the knowledge you've learned in this book to guide your search for a financial professional who will become one of the most important relationships that you'll maintain for the rest of your life.

CONCLUSION

YOUR PLAN, YOUR RETIREMENT, YOUR INCOME FOR LIFE

Everyone entering retirement faces the unknown. There is no way to avoid the fact that an uncertain future awaits you.

The good news is that many key factors *are* known, and these points of fact—some based on experience, some based on history, some based on simple math—represent enough of a framework of prediction that a plan taking those predictions into account is bound to set you up for success.

Your role as the retiree is not to become a market savant, nor is it to memorize the detailed minutiae of American tax law. Your role is not to hand over the keys to your retirement.

Your role as the retiree is simply to educate yourself, control the pieces within your control, seek help to maintain the more complicated parts, and put in the work to make your retirement goals a reality.

Having read this book, you are more than capable of developing the most important trait of a successful retiree: *discipline.* The best-structured plan in the world easily falls to ruin when the retiree strays from their discipline, allows emotional reactions to market downturns and volatility to cloud their thinking, and makes hasty, fear-based decisions. Your retirement is too important to allow it to fall apart; sticking to your plan should be your number one goal as you enter your distribution phase.

Qualified assistance from the outset is by far the most important step you can take to ensure a stress-free retirement that fulfills your goals. We wrote this book because we've watched thousands of clients move from a mindset of fear, reaction, anxiety, and avoidance to one of clarity and confidence, no matter their financial situation; we know that despite any fears you may have, you too are more than capable of achieving the same confidence. It's never too late to start. Use the tools in this book to take the first steps toward retirement; build a relationship with your financial planner to continue your journey.

When the big day arrives—when you can relax into retirement and step confidently into this new phase of your life—it will be with the knowledge that you are free to enjoy fully everything your retirement has to offer.

ABOUT THE AUTHORS

S. Joseph DiSalvo, ChFC, AIF and Marie L. Madarasz, AIF of Quest Capital & Risk Management, Inc. are committed to bringing their clients the clarity that will promote and enhance their confidence in the future.

For more than two decades they have used a proven process that helps clients think through how to best structure and manage their resources in order to produce a growing stream of retirement income for life. As experts specializing in all aspects of retirement income planning, they are passionate about the coordination and integration of their clients' income, investments, and tax planning strategies in order to help clients live the life they've worked hard for.

Joseph and Marie are strong advocates of financial education, seeking to teach others how to achieve sustained success and lifelong prosperity.